teen
Dream Jobs

How to find the job you REALLY want now!

---

by teen author Nora Coon

BEYOND
WORDS
Publishing
I   N   C

*To my parents and five elementary school teachers who let me write when
I should have been learning multiplication tables.*—Nora

Published by
Beyond Words Publishing, Inc.
20827 NW Cornell Road, Suite 500
Hillsboro, Oregon 97124
503-531-8700

Printed in the United States of America
Distributed to the book trade by Publishers Group West

Special Thanks To: Jenefer Angell, Kristen Getz, Elisa Libiran, Madeline Maxwell, Sarah
Minnich, Claire Nunez, Whitney Quon, and Kayt Zundel.

Library of Congress Cataloging-in-Publication Data

Coon, Nora.
  Teen dream jobs : how to get the job you really want now! / written by
Nora E. Coon.
    p. cm.
  Summary: A high school freshman shares insights, practical information,
and resources on conducting a job search and profiles other young
people, from twelve to seventeen years old, who have found their dream
jobs.
  ISBN 1-58270-093-1
  1. Job hunting--Juvenile literature. 2. Vocational guidance--Juvenile
literature. 3. Teenagers' writings, American. [1. Job hunting. 2.
Vocational guidance. 3. Youths' writings.] I. Title.

HF5392.C66 2003
650.14'0835—dc21
                                            2003041947

Contents

TM

Part 2: Dream Jobs You Can Get RIGHT NOW!

INTRODUCTION

What's Your Dream Job?

Think you have to wait till you're an adult to get a really cool job? Think your only choices for work are the occasional babysitting offer or working at the fast-food joint down the street? Well, think again. Whether it's working as a DJ at a local radio station, designing your own clothes, or test-marketing your new favorite video game, there is a cool job out there for you RIGHT NOW. Some of these jobs pay more than minimum wage, others might pay you and give you great fringe benefits, like discounts on movie tickets or clothes. But no matter what, by getting a job that really interests you, you'll be getting experience that will help you get other—even better—jobs later on.

The best way to get a job that you really enjoy is to base it on something you're good at, something you like, or something you do frequently. For example, if you love to play soccer, you can get a job coaching or refereeing kids' soccer games. That way, you can practice those impressive soccer moves, get to know other people who are serious about soccer, and earn money for your next pair of cleats. Or if you're interested in photography, you can get a job at a photo lab. Your coworkers can give you tips on creating great photos and you might even get a discount on your own developing. And if you're insanely devoted to hamburgers, you can always get a job in fast food—the possibilities are endless.

There are teens everywhere who have amazing jobs (you'll meet some of them in this book). Some had people who gave them some help, some had people who said their dreams were impossible, but all of them found ways to make it happen.

So how big can you dream? Imagine if waking up and going to work meant playing and critiquing those new video games that you could never afford to buy, reporting to the whole world how you feel about the president's foreign policy decisions, or seeing and reviewing the great movie that everyone's talking about.

You can do any one of those things or anything else that you've dreamed about! All it takes is some creativity, some goals, and a few tricks of the trade. This book is a good place to start. Read on to see how your talents and interests can lead you to the kind of work you'll love and for advice on landing the job you *really* want!

CHAPTER I

Discover Your Passion

THE "PERFECT" JOB

Although it may be true that there is one perfect person for you in this whole big world, the same does not apply to jobs. There is more than one perfect job out there just waiting for you to come along and snatch it up, but even the most exciting and glamorous jobs can have a boring or not-so-fun side. Actors have early mornings and often have to wait around. Working at a stable with horses can mean shoveling a lot of manure. Dancing can mean hours and hours of training—and less time for friends and fun. So, your job may not be wonderful all of the time, or even that great most of the time, but the trick is to find things about the job that interest you. Here's a good starting place for figuring out what might be perfect for you (at least right now):

Question Yourself

So you know that you really enjoy watching movies while eating Ben & Jerry's ice cream. Good! You know what you like, but how can you translate your love of movies and junk food into a real job? If you have no idea what your dream job might be, try asking yourself these key questions (keep in mind there are no right or wrong answers):

1. What do I like to do for fun?

2. Whom do I most admire? Why? What does she/he do for a living?

3. What is my most important achievement?

4. What is my happiest memory in school?

5. What is my favorite class? Why?

6. Where do I see myself ten years from now?

Now look at your answers. Do they share any similar themes? Are there any that feel exciting? Or make you wish for more? By simply looking at the similarities between your answers, you might discover the type of job, or at least the field or industry, that would make you the happiest.

Take Matters into Your Own Hands

Are you better suited to file paperwork or to chase three-year-olds around all day? Looking for a creative way to figure out your special skills? Career tests do the work for you! Check out these career quizzes available online, but remember, these are just quizzes—they shouldn't dictate what job you end up doing:

The Princeton Review Career Quiz
www.princetonreview.com/cte/quiz/default.asp

The Career Interests Game
www.career.missouri.edu/holland

The Career Key
www.careerkey.org/english/

You may not find your passion right away—in fact, it may take years—but you can still figure out what you like to do and what makes you happy. That way, every job can take you a little closer to your ultimate goal. No, you can't work as a veterinarian when you're a sophomore in high school, but you could work at a pet store or volunteer at a zoo.

Some jobs need a high level of training or education, but even when the training is over, employers will first look for people who have related experience. You can get some of that experience—and still have fun—if you find work in the field that's your passion. But there are also plenty of dream jobs that you don't have to wait for. Throughout this book, you'll learn the best tips for landing your dream job, see some ideas for fun jobs you can do right now, and meet other teens who are working in the world, doing what they love.

Teen Dream Job

Motivational Speaker and Instructor

Joshua Ballard
11 years old

1. How would you describe your job?
I am the President and CEO of Ballard International (www.ballard international.com). I am an instructor, a motivational public speaker, a photographer, a model, a Web site developer, and a graphic artist. As an instructor, each summer I teach a business class that I have designed entitled "Future Millionaires and Junior Entrepreneurs." During the past two years, I have taught this class at Cerritos College, Golden West College, Orange Coast College, Saddleback College, and California State University in Fullerton.

2. What do you teach in your classes?
Part of the curriculum of "Future Millionaires and Junior Entrepreneurs" is a personality test to help students determine which business best suits them. Then I offer the students about 125 business ideas to choose from. I help them customize a

business plan and discuss numerous marketing strategies to help their business succeed. On the last day of class, we have a business "expo" that gives the students the opportunity to launch their businesses, earn money, and obtain new customers.

3. How did you get your job?
I presented the curriculum for "Future Millionaires and Junior Entrepreneurs" to different colleges near my home. Soon, nine colleges offered to hire me to teach the class.

4. What is the most difficult part of your job?
Negotiating the fees for my services is the most difficult part of my job.

5. What is the most rewarding part of your job?
I love people. Meeting new people is the most rewarding part of my business. My students usually become my friends.

6. How do you balance spending time with friends and doing school work with your job?
My business does not take up a lot of my time. During the school year, I work from time to time on weekends as a speaker. My college teaching is done during the summer time.

7. How do you feel about school?
I strongly encourage kids and teen entrepreneurs to take their academic studies and learning seriously. As they learn, grow, meet new people, and explore different avenues of interest, the experiences they acquire will help them expand their business and earn more money.

8. What advice would you give to other kids searching for their dream jobs?
I would advise kids to do an inventory of their current hobbies and experiences. What are your academic strengths? Your favorite school subjects? What do you enjoy doing for fun? Where do you like to go? Find a need and fill it—the sky is the limit to what you can achieve.

Getting
Your Dream Job

CHAPTER 2

Finding Your Job

BEYOND THE CLASSIFIEDS

It's Sunday morning. You're wrestling your little brother for the comics when you suddenly realize: Hey, I should be looking through the classifieds for my new job. You open the paper to hundreds of ads: Web Site Designer; Music Store Clerk; Fast Food Service. Where to begin?

OK, there are definitely a lot of jobs out there that you are sure you DON'T want. So now it's time for you to search through all those job listings to find a job you DO want . . . or you can talk to friends and find out if they know anyone who's hiring. There are tons of great resources for tracking down a good job prospect. This chapter will show you some of them.

The Classifieds

There are many ways to make looking for a job easier than mulling over the classifieds for hours every day. To make the best use of your time, limit your job search in the classifieds to the local Sunday newspaper or try your paper's online version (see *Using the Internet*). The Sunday paper traditionally has the largest and most current job listings. Look for organized headings in the classifieds to make your search easier.

Once you've read through the classifieds, grab a pen and circle at least five job postings that match your experience and, ideally, relate to your dream job. You'll want to apply to these jobs as soon as possible, just to make sure that your application is at the top of the pile. Try to submit your application or resume by that following Monday or Tuesday.

Help Wanted Signs

There may be other jobs out there that aren't listed in newspapers. Walk or drive around your neighborhood and see if anyone has Help Wanted signs posted. If so, grab an application from the business and see if you can fill it out on the spot.

Sometimes managers don't realize they need the help until they meet the right person. If there's a business in your neighborhood that's a good fit for you, walk in and ask to speak to the manager. Introduce yourself and see if the owner is looking for help right now. Even if the business is not hiring at the moment, you can still leave your information on a resume in case someone needs it in the future (see Chapter 3 for resume writing tips).

Networking: Your Best Friend

So you've read classifieds until you can't see anymore. You've walked around looking for Help Wanted signs until you're exhausted and your legs are rubbery. There may be something you still haven't tried: networking. Opportunities pop up in very strange ways and often your own network of friends and family members can help you find a job.

Networking also means meeting and introducing yourself to new people who work in your area of interest. These people may know about job openings, have numbers for you to call, or give you the names of people to contact. Ask your family and friends if they know anyone who works in your target area or field. If they do, give them a copy of your resume and ask if they would please pass it on to their friend. The key to asking for networking help is to avoid being demanding. Remember, other people are doing you a favor by helping you find a job.

Using the Internet

Excited about being a camp counselor? Looking for a role as a movie extra? These specific interests may be hard to find in the classified section of your newspaper. You might have better luck trying the Internet. Read through online directories of jobs available for teenagers. Here's what to do:

◆ Visit Web sites that have information on jobs for teens (see the resource section in the back of this book).

◆ Check out online newspapers. Lots of newspaper classifieds are now on the Internet, so searching through the ads has gotten easier. You can search for your specific interests in their databases, with no fear of potential papercuts.

◆ Post resumes on search engines like Monster.com. (For safety reasons, make sure your resume doesn't include your home address. Include only your e-mail address or get a p.o. box).

Your search should result in finding lots of good Web sites related to your job interests. It may take a while to search through all the links, but when you find that perfect posting for "Day Camp Counselor" you'll be glad you took the time.

Make a List, Check it Twice

Now that you've completed your job search, list all the contact information for potential jobs. Remember to explore any job possibilities, not just your favorites. Don't be disappointed if you have to start at the bottom rung. Everyone has to start somewhere! Also, try to find as much as you can about each job. For example, some classified ads may not mention important details like pay scale or working hours.

After finding additional information on each job, organize your job prospects in a folder, ordering them from most desirable to least desirable. Even if nothing pans out, keep these notes for reference. It can be handy to

ℚUIZ: **What's the Best Way to Find a Job?**

1. You want to find a job, but you don't have any "connections." So you
a) open the newspaper to the classifieds, close your eyes, and randomly point to something. Who knows? You might get lucky.
b) spend fifteen minutes looking at all the small print, get dizzy, and decide to read the comics instead.
c) get out a red pen and circle the job leads that look interesting.

2. You've found a company that you'd like to intern for but you don't see anything on its Web site about internships. You
a) call the company and politely ask about unpaid internships.
b) decide that if the company wanted interns, it would say so—which means you haven't got a chance.
c) e-mail the company saying you'll work for $10 an hour; interested?

3. Your uncle has a law firm and he offers to help you network for a job. You
a) accept, but assume that he won't have any good leads.
b) thank him for his help and ask if he has any other job-searching advice.
c) forget to take him up on the offer and end up working at the local fast food joint.

4. You see an ad in the paper that sounds like a perfect job for you. You
a) call the company and say, "I want that job advertised in the paper. How much does it pay?"
b) send the company a letter and your resume, saying you're interested in the job.
c) go to the office and sit in the waiting room. Eventually someone will notice you're there and ask why.

5. You can't find anything in the local newspaper, so you
a) call your close relatives and let them know you're looking for a job.
b) apply for an out-of-state job, even though you're pretty sure your parents won't be willing to move across the country just because you found a minimum-wage job at a pet store.
c) give up. Who wants a job, anyway?

6. What are "the classifieds"?
a) a listing of jobs.
b) an encyclopedia index.

c) How should you know? That's the first part of the paper your mom throws in the recycling each morning.

7. In the middle of your job search, you notice an article in the paper about a new store that's just opened up. You
a) decide to stop by the store later that week.
b) don't care—you can't buy anything until you get a job!
c) call immediately and ask if they're hiring.

SCORING:
1. a=2, b=1, c=3
2. a=3, b=1, c=2
3. a=2, b=3, c=1
4. a=2, b=3, c=1
5. a=3, b=2, c=1
6. a=3, b=1, c=2
7. a=2, b=1, c=3

17–21 points:
Congratulations, you're on the right track! Remember: network, network, network. You'll be surprised who knows who and what doors will open. Don't forget to send thank-you notes, too!

12–16 points:
OK, you're trying, but it looks like you need a bit more help. You need to pay more attention to any and all leads—remember never to ignore a potential job opportunity!

7–11 points:
Job searching and networking isn't always easy, but in the end it's worth the extra effort. Just be sure to explore all your options and don't be afraid to try different approaches. You never know—success and fortune may be hiding under that unturned rock.

compare details and sometimes employers may contact you at a later date and you'll need to remember what the job was!

Call for details: Unless the ad specifically says "do not call," it's often a good idea to call first for more information. Try to find out as much as possible about the job—especially the hours you will be scheduled to work and what your responsibilities will be. There is no sense wasting the employer's time or your own by applying to a job that's not right for you; however, save questions about the pay for your interview. Employers are usually more interested in hiring people who are enthusiastic about the job and not only concerned about the money.

Contact information: Who is in charge of hiring for this position? Does the advertisement list a contact name? If not, try to get the name of the person responsible for hiring new employees. This information will be nice to have for your cover letter, thank you notes, and follow-up calls.

Common Teen Jobs

Though your first choice in your job search should be something that relates to your "perfect" job, sometimes just finding any job can be challenging. Here is a breakdown from the Bureau of Labor Statistics (2001) on the some top jobs for employed teens 16 to 19 years old:

Cashier: 13.7%
Stock handler and bagger: 5.7%
Cook: 5.6%
Wait staff: 4.2%
Sales worker: 3.4%
Food counter worker: 3.1%
Bus boy: 2.5%
Janitor and cleaner: 2%

But remember, this means that the other 59.8% aren't doing these jobs.

Dangerous Teen Jobs

As you're applying to jobs, you may want to avoid these risky jobs for teens—or at least do some careful research before accepting a position.

Driving jobs: These include operating a forklift or other motorized equipment. (You usually have to be over eighteen for these jobs.)

Working by yourself: Working by yourself in a convenience store or at a fast food establishment can be risky. Often these businesses are targets for robbery and other crime. Check with your local police for statistics to see if the business you want to work for is high risk.

Cooking: Working with items like hot grease, boiling water, high temperature cooking surfaces, sharp knives, and restaurant-size appliances make cooking more dangerous work.

Heavy work: This includes construction, commercial fishing, and landscaping. Since these jobs often involve working at heights, in the ocean, or with heavy equipment, they can also pose safety risks.

OK, you're all ready to go find your job. Aside from actually getting the job, this can be the best part of all. You get to imagine yourself in all kinds of positions and picture what it would really be like to work as whatever you want. By now you should know that the classifieds aren't the only way to find your job. You've got those wonderful Help Wanted signs (watch for them everywhere you go), networking (always thank anyone who gives you a job lead), and the wonderful, wonderful invention called the Internet (just make sure the job postings are legitimate). Get going and find that job!

Teen Dream Job

Professional DJ

Andrew Collins
14 years old

1. How did you become interested in being a DJ?
My cousin Bobby really introduced me to the art of the disc jockey. I was down in his basement one time, and he started demonstrating his lighting effects and music-mixing skills. Red lasers made patterns on the floor; the bass was thumping. It evoked a feeling in me, lots of energy, and positive vibes. I was definitely hooked.

2. How long have you DJ-ing?
In the spring of 1999 I bought myself a "DJ starter set" with all the money I had saved from past Christmases and birthdays. It consisted of two turntables and a simple two-channel mixer so I could blend the songs together. I got some records and started messing around. It took a while for anything that sounded decent to come out, but I was having a lot of fun, so I kept at it. From that point on, I just started practicing and adding equipment whenever I could afford it.

3. What is the most challenging part of what you do?

It's tough to keep everyone in a crowd happy. Everybody has their own taste in music, especially in a setting like a high school dance, so you can't just sit there and play one kind of music—even your own favorites— for three hours. You have to make sure everyone gets a little bit of what they like. I mean, most of the music for a dance is going to be dance music (hip-hop, techno) but you've also got to throw in some rock, some real bubble-gum pop, and some slower grooves for the people who like that stuff.

4. What is the best part of your job?

The best part of being a DJ is when you get positive crowd response. When the whole floor is moving to your beats and you're controlling the dance and all the gyrations with your mixing board, you know you're doing something great. I'm an entertainer; I want people to feel the groove and go crazy.

5. What work does your job consist of?

Performing and playing music is a large part of my job, but there are many "behind the scenes" elements involved that aren't quite so glamorous. I also have to deal with contracts, bookings, knowing which dates I can play and which I can't for family reasons or a big cross-country race the next day or whatever.

6. How did you get your dream job?

You have to make yourself known; you have to get your name to the right people. I put up flyers, made business cards and handed them out, and talked to people all the time about what I was doing. A huge percentage of business I do comes from word of mouth. If I do well at a gig and the client's friend needs a DJ, the network kicks into action.

7. Who helped you along the way?

I couldn't have gotten to the point where I am without my family. Starting out, I constantly asked my cousin for advice on equipment and technique. I still have questions for him every now and then—he's in college and still performing too. I also get great support from my parents. My dad serves as my "roadie," helping me with loading/unloading equipment, driving me to gigs in the family minivan, and helping me set up at the gig.

8. How do you balance school and friends with your job?

I work pretty hard not to let schoolwork pile up. If I can make progress on a big project during a study hall, I do. I'm in some honors-level classes where teachers pile on the work and expect it to be done. I also run cross-country, which actually helps.

During a hard run I can think about all kinds of things: the job, schoolwork, and business that needs to be taken care of.

9. What advice would you give to other kids searching for their dream jobs?
Try to find something you love, because if you don't love your job you won't do it well. And definitely learn from your mistakes. I've made many, but I've definitely learned a lot along the way. It's also important not to get discouraged when things don't go your way. Remember that you've got to give it your all to make it a success, and that's a lot easier if you're wild for what you're doing.

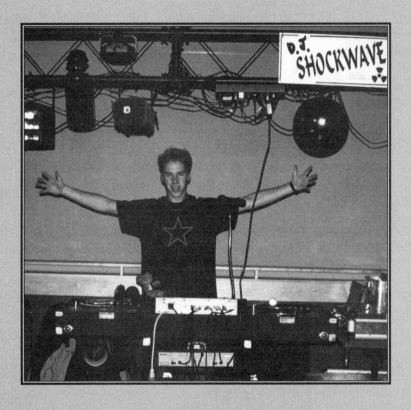

CHAPTER 3

It's All About You

WRITING A SAVVY RESUME & COVER LETTER

So, you sit down at your computer, ready to write your resume. You stare at the screen, trying to think. And stare. And then it comes to you—you have no idea what to put in your resume! How on earth are you supposed to write one?

Resume comes from the French word that means "summary." Basically, a resume is a summary of why you're the best person for a particular job. This chapter has all the information you'll need to come up with an awesome resume—one that will really impress employers and land you the job of your dreams—as well as information on cover letters and getting good references.

Why Are Resumes Important?

You may ask, "Why should I bother with a resume? I'm just applying for a job as a referee (or bookstore clerk, or camp counselor, or whatever)." Items like a resume, cover letter, and personal recommendations can give you an extra edge when applying for a job. You can put a lot of important details on your resume that employers may not ask for on your job application.

Essential Resume Items

Here are some key headings that you'll want to include on your resume:

Contact information: It's very important to list your name and contact information (address, phone number, e-mail) on the resume so that your future employer can get in touch with you about the job. The standard location for this information is at the top of your resume.

Objective: The objective (the reason you want the job) should be right below your name and contact information. By including an objective you're letting your future employer know exactly why you want this particular job. (You can also include this information in your cover letter.)

Education: You should include information on your school, what grade you're in, your GPA (optional), and what classes (high school or community college) you've taken that relate to the job.

Experience: Any experience, no matter how small, should be put on your resume. This includes work experience as well as work you've done for family members, internships, volunteering, and job-related hobbies or other interests. This lets your employer know why you're qualified for the job or why you should be considered and that you're a well-rounded person.

Computer skills: Many jobs require computer experience, so it's an added bonus to list any computer or software know-how.

References: Make a note that these are available on request but don't include them on your resume.

Additional Resume Headings

Your resume should be about a page long. If adding any of the following information makes it too long, try shortening what you have or using a format that will allow you to squeeze in the most information.

Interests/extracurricular activities: After-school activities like sports, debate club, chess club, and volunteering can show off your varied interests and highlight your other talents.

Languages spoken: Since many employers are looking for people who are bilingual, detailing your language skills is another added bonus for your resume.

Awards: List any awards to show what a wonderful, intelligent, talented person you are!

Writing Your Resume

Wondering what's resume-worthy? Here's how you figure it out. Write everything you did after school and over the summer:

Now think about how you can make your activities apply to work experience. List your most impressive experience in chronological order.

You can use active verbs to refer to your work. Here are some examples:

- ◆ organized
- ◆ instituted
- ◆ created
- ◆ helped

If you find yourself still running short on things to say, be sure to include hobbies, school responsibilities, and activities as well as other experience like babysitting, berry picking, lawn mowing, or volunteering, community service, or extracurricular activities.

Chronological or Functional?

There are two basic types of resumes, chronological and functional. On the following pages, you can see examples of both. A chronological resume organizes your work experience by the dates that you've worked, beginning with your most recent work experience. In a functional resume, instead of organizing the resume by dates, the resume is organized by how relevant your work experience is to the job you're applying for. If you've done a lot of odd jobs like babysitting and lawn-mowing, or if you've had one job over a long period of time, a functional resume might work better for you.

That's One Good-Looking Resume!

Once you've chosen the type of resume you want, you'll need to choose a style for your resume. If you have access to a computer with Microsoft Word, you can use the resume templates and a "Resume Wizard" that allows you to pick the style of your resume as well as the headings.

If you don't want to use this program or don't have it, you can easily create your own resume format. The key to formatting a good-looking resume is to make it easy to read.

Paper: When it comes to paper, go with a white or neutral color and a slightly heavier stock. Sometimes fancy or brightly-colored paper can be distracting, not to mention expensive, and can make the print hard to read.

SAMPLE: Chronological Resume

K. Smith
5230 Apple Blossom Ln.
Portland, OR 95555
Phone: (503) 555-5555
E-mail: ksmith@soccer.ie

Objective: To obtain a referee position with the Portland Youth Soccer League.

Education:
Junior, Hamilton High School   *2001-present*
Portland, OR
* 3.9 GPA
* Captain/Goalie, Hamilton Hornets Soccer Team

Experience:
Peer Mediator   *2001-present*
Hamilton High School   Portland, OR
* Mediated disputes between peers using anti-aggression techniques
* Ran series of anger-management workshops at school
* Created new mediation system that decreased adult involvement by 40%

Sports Editor   *2001-present*
The Hamilton Chronicle, Hamilton High School   Portland, OR
* Covered over 100 sports events per year
* Edited sports section of the *Hamilton Chronicle*
* Wrote weekly soccer column, "Katarine's Kicks"

Volunteer Coach   *2001-present*
Oregon At-Risk Children's Soccer League   Portland, OR
* Taught soccer rules to 20 children ages 6-10, including 3 with ADD
* Helped with transportation to and from games across state
* Acted as volunteer referee & mediated player disputes

Interests: Soccer, Journalism, and Spanish.

Awards:
* 2002 Youth Soccer Player of the Year, State of Oregon
* 2001 Youth Soccer Player of the Year, State of Oregon

SAMPLE: Functional Resume

J. Corliss
66 W Way, Apt. 3A
Schenectady, NY 10267
Phone (224) 555-5555
E-mail: jcorliss@mail.ie

Objective: To obtain a summer position at KidzAfterSkool day care.

Education:
Junior, Schenectady Regional High School   *2001-present*
Schenectady, NY

Summary of Qualifications:
4 years of experience with children ages 3–11
2 years of experience with leadership of peers & younger children
Solid communications background

Childcare Experience:
Babysat with Neighborhood Kid-Sitters

Leadership Experience:
Lead 15 boys ages 9–10 through summer camp
Started Neighborhood Kid-Sitters

Communications Experience:
Wrote an article on volunteer work for *SRH Journal* (school newspaper)
Wrote fillers for *At-Risk Children's League* newspaper
Proofread & edited articles for *At-Risk Children's League* newspaper

Languages:
5 years of Spanish

References:
Available upon request

Fonts: Your resume should be typed (not handwritten). You will need to choose a very readable font such as Times or Palatino. Not everyone has perfect vision and few employers will spend the extra time trying to decipher an artistic or unique font on your resume.

Style: You can use design features like bold headings and bullets to highlight important details on your resume, though overdoing it might make it confusing to read so try to keep it simple. Make sure everything is consistent—fonts, periods, spaces—and make sure your resume has the correct grammar and punctuation before you send it in. Attention to detail is important.

Resume Don'ts

Lastly, there are a few important pitfalls to writing a resume that you want to avoid:

Lying about your experience: This may seem obvious, but you really want to be as honest as possible on your resume. Your employer might double-check your resume information. If you get hired, it will be clear once you get the job that you were fudging the facts. You could even get fired for lying or not knowing what you're doing.

Mistakes: It's OK if you make a mistake on your resume, but try to avoid fixing it with an ink pen. It's worth printing out a new, clean copy of the resume. Only if you notice a big mistake right when you're about to turn in the resume (like your name is misspelled or your phone number has an extra digit) should you go for an ink pen correction.

T.M.I.: That's right, putting too much information on your resume can sometimes work against you. Avoid listing tons of superfluous information about yourself that is not relevant to your experience or the job you're applying for. Try to keep it to one side of one page and you should be just fine.

Hold the Applause until the End

As you can see, the best part about writing a resume is that you can summarize all your skills and everything you've done (even if it's just small things like putting together projects for school or odd jobs around your neighborhood) to make your experience look really good. That, by the way, is a really important skill: knowing how to show all your accomplishments in a favorable light. Employers are looking for proof that you will be able to handle the job, and a good resume reflects any and all work experience (even if it is unpaid). This information will help the employer decide whether to take a chance on you.

Cover Letters

Now that you have your resume, you're ready to write an impressive cover letter—the letter that you send with your resume to introduce yourself—that will convince employers to immediately pick up the phone and call you for an interview! Cover letters are an important part of the application process.

Unfortunately, when you send prospective employers a cover letter, they are only seeing a small side of your personality. Your cover letter will be your employer's "first impression" of you. For this reason, your letter needs to convey some important information about you in just a short amount of space. Here are some quick tips for making cover letters brief, to the point, and interesting for your future boss:

◆ Keep the letter short. It should be no more than three to four paragraphs long, and no more than one page.
◆ Personalize your letter to the person hiring. This will help get his or her attention. If you don't know the person's name, open with "To whom it may concern."
◆ Focus on why the company should hire you and what you can bring to the company.
◆ Persuade the employer that you're really a quality worker. Then make sure

QUIZ: Resume and Cover Letter Ready?

1. A resume is
a) some weird French word. Besides, you took Spanish, so how should you know?
b) a kind of chocolate.
c) a document that lists your qualifications for a job.

2. Your resume should be
a) handwritten or typed, it doesn't matter.
b) typed.
c) done as a music video.

3. The paper your resume is on should be
a) colored and perfumed.
b) beige, light gray, or white, and slightly heavier than regular printer paper.
c) paper? Why would you need paper for a music video?

4. When you ask someone for a recommendation, you should say,
a) "Write me a recommendation. Send it to me by Tuesday."
b) "I need you to write lots of nice stuff about me by tomorrow."
c) "Would you be willing to write me a recommendation?"

5. When writing a resume, you should
a) include plenty of good information, such as volunteer experience and the dates that you worked for other employers.
b) make up extra stuff so that you sound really impressive. It's not like they'll bother to check up on you.
c) be sure to include photos of your prizewinning pet pig (even though she has nothing to do with the job your applying for).

6. Your resume
a) should impress the person reading it with your professional attitude and make him or her want to hire you.
b) should show how creative you are by using lots of colors and shapes and weird fonts.
c) is a total waste of time. No one cares about it anyway.

7. A "cover letter" is
a) a plastic sheath you slide a letter into.
b) a short letter included with your resume, explaining who you are and why you want the job.
c) a wool blanket that covers your resume to keep it from getting cold.

SCORING:

1. a=2, b=1, c=3
2. a=2, b=3, c=1
3. a=2, b=3, c=1
4. a=2, b=1, c=3
5. a=3, b=2, c=1
6. a=3, b=2, c=1
7. a=2, b=3, c=1

17–21 points:

Excellent work! You know lots about writing a resume and cover letter already, so check out the sample resumes in this chapter to see how yours compares.

12–16 points:

You understand some aspects of resume and cover letter writing, but you could use a bit more practice. Ask an experienced adult to check your work and give you feedback on it. Before you know it, you'll have a dream job in no time!

7–11 points:

OK, time to get started! After all, resumes and covers letters aren't as hard as they may seem. Follow the advice in this chapter, stay focused on your most impressive skills and experience, and be sure to ask for proofreading help from friends and family.

to back it up with the evidence (i.e., internships, previous jobs, volunteer work) that's listed on your resume.

◆ Avoid writing anything negative about yourself. No matter how minor, this may give the employer a reason not to consider you for the position.

Breaking It Down: Cover Letters Made Easy

Here is a rough outline for your cover letter:

Paragraph 1: The first paragraph should explain to your prospective employer which job you are applying for and why you should be considered for the position.

Paragraph 2: Your second paragraph can give more detailed reasons for why you want to work for this company and what the company will gain from hiring you.

Paragraph 3: In the third paragraph, you can point to your resume and briefly highlight any experience that qualifies you for the job.

Paragraph 4: The last paragraph should be short and sweet. Conclude your letter with just a sentence or two thanking the employer for his or her consideration.

Recommendations

Besides resumes and cover letters, part of the application process usually requires that you provide recommendations from people who know you. These are the people who agree to tell a possible employer what a terrific person you are and why he or she should hire you. Generally you want to avoid getting recommendations from parents or other family members. Good people to ask for recommendations include former bosses, volunteer supervisors, friends of your parents, teachers, and anyone else who really loved your work or whom you enjoyed working with.

Contacting References

Wondering how to ask for recommendations? Call or e-mail the person you'd like to list and tell her or him that you're applying for a job or internship. Then ask if he or she would be willing to write you a recommendation. Here is a sample letter:

Dear _____;

I'm now applying for a job with _____. Would you be willing to write me a recommendation?

Many thanks,
You

Be sure to ask your references before listing them on your resume. It can be awkward to list a former teacher on your resume as a reference, only to find out that she doesn't remember who you are or what class she had you in. Once you've been in touch with your references and have their permission, list their names, titles, companies/organizations/schools, and phone numbers on a reference sheet. Here's an example:

Karen Jackson, Manager
Smith Super Saver
Phone: (555) 555-5555 ext. 106
E-mail: kjackson@supersaver.usa
Available 2–6 P.M. weekdays

The Best Information

Now, all this may seem like a lot of information, but don't worry! Resumes and cover letters aren't that hard to write, and they're only one piece of your job experience. True, they are an important part, but they're still only one part. Don't freak out if your resume feels boring or plain or really, really empty—employers don't expect you to be perfect. They just hope to have the best information to decide if you're right for the job.

Teen Dream Job

Artist and Entrepreneur

Mary Catherine Lindsay
14 years old

1. How did you become interested in creating your own stationery company?
I became interested in stationery because of my interest in art. Stationery is a great way for me to pursue my love of art and enter into the business world.

2. Describe a typical day at work.
Since my job at Grasshopper Press is to draw the designs, I do most of my work at home. Fortunately, I do not need to draw every day. I just draw when I have an idea, when I'm inspired, or when I am just bored.

3. What is the most challenging part of your work?
One of the hardest parts of owning Grasshopper Press is drawing designs that are not particularly for my age group. Drawing designs for adults, boys, and young children is something that is a bit foreign to me.

4. What is the most rewarding part of your work?
The best thing about having Grasshopper Press is being able to see that people enjoy

my work. If it puts a smile on their face, it surely puts one on mine. I hope that my work will brighten up people's days and inspire them too.

5. How do you balance work with school and friends?
Balancing my schedule is still a skill I have yet to master, but normally I can keep school, work, friends, and activities in their respective places. Sometimes it's hard not to draw in class, but when I doodle, I doodle for a purpose! I have learned how convenient it is to have friends around to ask for new ideas.

6. What advice would you give other kids and teens searching for their dream jobs?
My advice is this: follow your dreams. Your love and interests will be the fire in what you do. Also, do not forget to get help from family and friends. Their feedback can give you a good idea of what a customer would like.

Mary Catherine Drew

www.grasshopperpress.com

Samantha Michelle

CHAPTER 4

Sweaty Hands and Bad Outfits

THIS ISN'T A DATE; IT'S YOUR FIRST INTERVIEW!

You go into the office, sit down across from the interviewer, gulp, and hand them your resume. The interviewer looks at it, then at you, then bursts into hysterical laughter. You panic and run. Then you realize—you're wearing your sister's clown costume!

Your interview doesn't have to be that bad! Interviews aren't designed to intimidate you; they're meant to help the employer determine if you're right for the job. Don't be discouraged if you don't get the first job you interview for. It just means there's something better for you out there. Know yourself, your strengths, weaknesses, and preferences. Try to determine what you want out of the company and what the company expects of you. Remember, you have to put yourself out there and take some risks to get the job of your dreams.

How to Keep Your Career Cool: Interview Basics

Think positive: It's hard not to walk into an interview dreading the worst. To keep your body language on a positive note, show confidence (even if you don't feel it), try to stay calm, and remain open, friendly, and polite with the interviewer. Avoid any negative thoughts or comments as this could suggest to the interviewer that you are a negative person.

Nonverbal communication: You may not know it, but nonverbal communication is a huge part of the interview process. Nervous twitches, playing with your hair, slouching, and not looking the interviewer in the eyes can sometimes reveal more about how you feel than what you say in the interview. By making eye contact with the interviewer you're conveying a sense of honesty and professionalism.

Prepare yourself: Practice interviewing with friends and family and try answering different questions that might arise. Before your interview, make an effort to arrive 10 to 15 minutes ahead of time and remember to bring an up-to-date, clean copy of your resume and references in case the interviewer asks for them.

Keep calm: There are lots of ways to relax and keep calm before an interview. Deep breathing, stretches, yoga, herbal teas, if you like them, are all good ideas. Once you're in your interview, don't be afraid to ask for a glass of water or to use the restroom if you need to.

Special schedules: If you are applying for a summer job and you know that your family is leaving for a week to stay with your grandparents in Florida, be sure to go to the interview with the exact dates. Employers appreciate knowing these details before they hire you and it's not always easy for new hires to get time off if it hasn't been arranged in advance.

The bottom line: It's best to let the interviewer bring up the rate of pay; however, if the interview seems to be ending, it's OK to ask about it. Just don't let it seem like this is all that you're interested in (even if it is!).

Mock Interview

Want to practice interviewing? The following is a sample interview script. Grab a friend and take turns being the interviewer and the job applicant. If you can't get a friend to help you, ask your parents or siblings. You may feel silly at first, but you'll be glad that you prepared. If you have access to a video camera, ask someone to record your mock interview so that you can watch it later on. You may notice that you slouch or that you have some nervous habits, like avoiding eye contact, to watch out for.

Interview Script

After arriving 10 to 15 minutes early, you walk confidently into the interviewer's office wearing your best pair of pants, shoes, and nice button-down shirt. You shake hands firmly with the interviewer and smile as you greet her.

Interviewer: Hello, you must be my five o'clock interview.

You: Yes, I'm _____. It's great to meet you.

Interviewer: Well, I've looked at your resume, and you've certainly done some interesting things for someone your age.

You: I've been fortunate to have a lot of great experiences. (List some examples).

Interviewer: I'm impressed. Why do you want to work at our company?

You: I'm really interested in working here. I've spent my summers coming here since I was a child. It really feels like the right place for me after my work as a (something you've done) and (something you've done).

Interviewer: What do you consider your strengths to be?

You: I feel that some of my strengths are working with people and being very organized.

QUIZ: Are You Prepared for Your First Interview?

1. You're interviewing for a job at a local clothing store. When you're getting dressed, you grab
a) a nice pair of pants and a collared shirt.
b) a black hoodie, torn black pants with random patches cut out, a nose ring, an eyebrow ring, and a pair of combat boots. If they can't accept your individuality, why work for them?
c) sweats. Why not be comfortable?

2. You just got back from a run and have to get ready for your job interview later that day. You decide to
a) grab a bottle of cologne/perfume off the shelf and douse yourself in it.
b) take a shower and be sure to reach for the deodorant. No gymn smell for you!
d) skip the shower and forget to brush your teeth. Smell? What smell?

3. When you get to the office for your interview, you're ten minutes late. You
a) stroll into your interview like nothing happened. Maybe the interviewer will think she got the time wrong.
b) make sure you're breathing hard as you run in, so the interviewer will know you really did want to be there on time, you just . . . well, you just weren't.
c) apologize for inconveniencing her and honestly explain the reason why you were late.

4. The interview is going well, and you want to ask about money and benefits. You say
a) "How much does this position usually pay? Are there any additional job benefits?"
b) "What's in it for me?"
c) nothing. They'll bring it up once they're comfortable talking about it. Instead you sit quietly and listen.

5. When you walk into the interviewer's office, she has a UCLA pennant on the wall. You ask if she went to UCLA, and she says yes. You
a) tell her your sister is going there in the fall (she is) and ask how the interviewer liked it.
b) gush that you really want to go to UCLA too! (Even though you know you have no intention of applying there).
c) nod disinterestedly—UCLA is just another college to you.

6. You're very nervous about this interview—you desperately want the job. So you
a) spend a few hours playing Xbox to avoid thinking about it.
b) drink some coffee to make sure you'll be wide awake for the interview, since you didn't get any sleep last night.
c) make sure you have everything ready for your interview, then breathe deeply and remind yourself of all the preparation you've put into this—you won't fail.

7. You're pretty sure the interview went well. But when you don't hear from the company for a couple days, you
a) decide they don't want you and give up. Who wants a job, anyway?
b) write the interviewer a short thank-you letter that asks if he has made a decision.
c) call and demand an explanation.

Scoring:
1. a=3, b=1, c=2
2. a=2, b=3, c=1
3. a=1, b=2, c=3
4. a=3, b=1, c=2
5. a=3, b=2, c=1
6. a=1, b=2, c=3
7. a=2, b=3, c=1

17–21 points:
Nice work! You get how to interview and you know that it's OK to be a little nervous. You're gonna do great at your first interview. Good luck!

12–16 points:
These people are hiring you, not marrying you; ease up a little. It's great that you want to feel so prepared, but you're actually hurting your cause when you try too hard. Relax and remember, even if this interview doesn't go well, there's always the next one.

7–11 points:
OK, everyone has off days. Maybe Xbox relaxes you, but you *do* want to make sure you're ready for the interview *before* you start goofing off. Give yourself plenty of time to practice and prepare, and you'll do just fine.

Interviewer: Do you have any questions?

You: Yes. Can you tell me a little about the typical work day here?

Interviewer: Of course. (Gives details).

You: That sounds very interesting. Can you tell me what the position pays?

Interviewer: Oh, we haven't covered that, have we? (Gives details). Do you have any other questions?

You: No, I think you've covered just about everything. It sounds like a great position.

Interviewer: Well, thanks for coming in. We'll contact you in the next few days to let you know if you've gotten the job.

You: Thank you. (Stand up, smile, shake hands, and exit.)

Notice that money was discussed only after you had a chance to show your enthusiasm for the position. Though not all interviews will go this smoothly, simply preparing yourself can help you feel more calm and confident in an interview.

How to Dress for Success

What you wear to an interview depends on the type of job you're trying to get. As a general rule, dress nicely, in a button-down shirt and non-denim long pants without holes. Watch out for wearing anything too flashy or casual. The employer will be more interested in whether you are neat and presentable than whether you look good. Even if the job you are applying for is messy, hard labor, dressing with care gives the employer the message that you really want the job.

Shirts: Choose a clean shirt. Guys, it's a good idea to tuck your shirt in; girls, you can go either way. Avoid shirts with holes, stains, and any written statements or controversial pictures. Skip anything that's see-through, too tight, or shows a whole lot of skin.

Pants/skirts: Slacks are usually best, because you don't want to look too casual, but you can also wear dark jeans, nice khakis, or black pants. Make sure the pants aren't too low or too tight. Skirts should never be shorter than a few inches above your knee.

Shoes: Wear nice shoes. If you truly can't find anything, black sneakers are OK. But if you have nothing but gross sandals, borrow some of your mom's or dad's shoes.

Jewelry: Earrings are fine and so is other jewelry as long as you don't go overboard. Flashy or garish jewelry can be distracting to the interviewer. As far as piercings go, unless you've just had your ears pierced and cannot take the earrings out, one earring in each ear is the general rule. Other visible body piercings—like your nose, chin, or eyebrow—can also be distracting, and you'll probably want to take them out as well.

Other: Some makeup is OK. Avoid cologne or perfume, or if you can't resist, wear only a microscopic amount. No matter how great you think it is, lots of people are allergic to the smelly stuff.

Of course, a lot of these rules are flexible depending on the job. If you want a job in a store that caters to the rocker-chick or pierced crowd, you can wear something a little different from what you'd wear to an interview at a fine restaurant where the patrons are dressed conservatively.

Things to Avoid

Being late: Arriving to an interview late is the easiest way to turn a good first impression into a bad one. If there's a choice between wasting precious minutes debating over the perfect outfit for your interview or arriving on time, getting there on time is more likely to land you the job.

Bad grooming: So you have the perfect pant-shirt combo for your interview, but your hair is a wild disaster and you have dirt under your nails. Employers are looking at the whole package, so don't forget basic grooming when you go for your interview.

Extra baggage: Carrying lots of bags, paper, or other items into the interview could distract you and the interviewer. Just carry what you need.

Thank-You Letters

After your interview, it's always a good idea to follow-up (the next day!) with a thank-you note. Your thank-you letter should sound genuine and reflect your appreciation in being considered for the job. Here are the basics you'll want to include:

1.) State that you enjoyed meeting the interviewer and appreciate the time taken to meet with you.

2.) Explain that after the interview, you are still very much interested in working for the company.

3.) Highlight any important skills you have that you may have forgotten to mention in the interview.

4.) Thank the interviewer again and give him or her your contact information—just in case it was misplaced.

Congratulations!

You've survived your first interview—the good and the bad. You managed the outfit, the "baggage," the nerve-wracking questions . . . everything! Hopefully you'll get the job, but even if you don't, you've learned something from the experience. Your next interview will go even better.

Teen Dream Job

Professional Musician

Christopher Ballard
12 years old

1. What kind of work do you do?
I am a violinist, pianist, and music composer.

2. How did you become interested in playing the violin and composing?
I love music. I started to play the violin at age 6 and the piano at age 7. I excelled soon after I began taking lessons. My love for music has opened the door to wonderful opportunities.

3. How did you get your dream job in music?
At age 8, I was invited to be the guest artist at a Christmas luncheon. Everyone was amazed with my performance and many of the guests recommended that I perform at other events. So I started playing for churches, fundraising events, corporate functions, galas, and national conventions. Today, I have performed in hundreds of pres-

tigious events, including a solo violin performance for President George W. Bush's inaugural festivities.

4. What is the most rewarding part of your job?
Being a performer allows me to travel to exciting places and meet wonderful people.

5. How do you balance spending time on school work with your job?
In addition to doing my homework, I practice regularly during the week to prepare for performances. I usually work on weekends.

6. What advice would you give to other kids searching for their dream jobs?
Don't be afraid to explore, seek the help of successful adults who are willing to assist you, and dream big. Write down your goals and work toward your goals. I am currently writing a book to share my experiences with other kids and to share many successful tips that have helped me. Basically, the purpose of my new book is to inspire young people to succeed.

7. What are your future goals?
After performing solo at President Bush's inauguration, he asked to meet privately with my family. I was inspired by the president when he said that my brother or I could one day become president of the United States.

    Since meeting with the president, I have taken a more serious approach to politics. Now, I have decided to go to law school, become an attorney, pursue a career in politics and later (when I am 35 years old) run for the office of president. When I perform, I often share my political hopes with my fans and I ask them to please vote for me when I run for office—23 years from now! I strongly believe that this is a reachable goal.

For more information about Christopher visit: **www.ChristopherBallard.com**

CHAPTER 5

Nobody's Hiring

INTERNSHIPS AND OTHER WORK EXPERIENCE

You've spent the last month searching for a job, and you're desperate to get some experience—but nobody seems to want to hire a teenager. Don't worry, there are lots of options out there! You can intern, take classes, or volunteer to get work experience . . . big opportunities await those who don't insist on getting paid.

Getting Paid Isn't Everything

What if no one is interested in hiring teenagers? Does your resume have to stay blank and empty? There are lots of ways to boost your resume and fill your summer even if you can't get a job. Money isn't everything and internships or volunteer work can be a great ways to get experience, make contacts, and maybe figure out exactly what you want to do in your life. Plus, sometimes an internship or volunteering can eventually lead to paid work with the same company!

What's an Internship?

An internship differs from a summer or part-time job in that it is educational work experience, often unpaid. An internship can be compared with an apprenticeship. It may include assisting a professional with day-to-day activities or completing special projects. Every intern can expect to perform some clerical or routine duties, but these activities should not constitute the bulk of the student's time. Students perform internships in industries as diverse as entertainment, health care, retailing, law, and government.

Finding Internships

"OK," you're saying, "you've convinced me, so how the heck do I get an internship?" Here are some ideas:

Cold calls: This method assumes you already know where your interests lie and you know a couple of companies that you'd like to intern with. Call or e-mail them and mention that you're a student interested in an internship.

Internship directory: Refer to an internship directory at you local library and find an internship that interests you. Make sure it's somewhere you can get to (like in your same city). Turn to the section of stuff you're interested in and start reading. Then send a cover letter explaining why you want to intern with the company (along with your resume) to those companies that look interesting.

Contacts: Ask around to see who your friends and family know in the fields you are interested in, then see if you can find yourself an internship through their connections.

Experience: What's the best thing you can do to prepare yourself for an internship? Do something related to it first. If you're interested in a film internship, you don't have to go out and make a movie, but you have to have experience, such as having taken a filmmaking class. If you want a

QUIZ: Do You Have Intern Potential?

1. You've accepted the fact that you might not get the paying job you want, so you
a) halfheartedly research a couple of internships and volunteer opportunities but give up at the first sign of difficulty.
b) mope around at home, finally deciding that maybe you should never have tried to get a job in the first place.
c) go out and find yourself a terrific internship. If that company didn't want you, it's their loss!

2. You've arranged an internship with an automechanic. The first day of work, you
a) follow the mechanic around silently, mentally complaining that it'd be much more fun to get paid for all of this.
b) ask a couple questions about radiators and transmissions, but are otherwise pretty quiet.
c) get totally into it, helping the mechanic with all his tools, even working on the engine of a 60s Mustang that you'd love to own someday.

3. It's your first day volunteering at the Humane Society. You didn't really want to be a volunteer, but they don't take rescue workers under 18 (something about "potential for injury"). You
a) work hard and enjoy it. At the end of the day, you have to admit that you've learned a lot and still feel the satisfaction of helping improve an animal's life.
b) spend the whole day thinking about how boring it is to just feed the animals, rather than saving lives.
c) try to keep an open mind about things and to make the most of the experience, even though you can't help thinking about how you wanted to do more.

4. You love birds and find an exciting job at the Audubon Society. Then you discover the job is an unpaid, volunteer position. You
a) change your mind. Who wants to work for free?
b) try it out even though you'd rather find something that pays.
c) accept the position and work as hard as you can to get the most out of it.

5. When you're looking for an internship, you
a) ask your mom if you can intern where she works.
b) read the classifieds, then pick out a random company, call, and say, "I want to intern with you. How much will you pay me?"
c) consider what you're really interested in, research three or four possible internships, and then call or e-mail to inquire about unpaid internships.

6. You're thinking about this whole not-getting-paid thing, and it sounds
a) terrible! Isn't the whole point to earn some money?
b) bearable, if not great. Yeah, you want money, but if this is the only way to get experience . . .
c) definitely cool if it means you can work wherever you want. You have to admit that getting paid is fun, but an interesting job can be just as much fun.

7. You've come to the end of your volunteer job, and as you look back on it, you think
a) What a waste of time! I could have been making money—I could own ten new CDs by now.
b) Awesome! I can't wait till next year!
c) Well, it was OK, but I'm never doing that again.

SCORING
1. a=2, b=1, c=3
2. a=1, b=2, c=3
3. a=3, b=1, c=2
4. a=1, b=2, c=3
5. a=2, b=1, c=3
6. a=1, b=2, c=3
7. a=1, b=3, c=2

17–21 points:
Great! You understand that interning and volunteering can open a ton of opportunities for you that a lot of paying jobs really can't. Go out there, volunteer or intern, and don't forget to put your new experience on your resume!

12–16 points:
OK, you're a little hesitant, but you'd still take a chance and consider volunteering or interning. Remember, your future employers will want someone with experience.

7–11 points:
Well, internships and volunteering sound sorta interesting to you, but that not-getting-paid part really bugs you . . . . But instead of getting lots of great experience, you might be stuck at home, watching daytime TV. Internships and volunteering can provide that extra experience that can eventually lead to a great paying job. Sometimes, getting paid isn't the most important thing.

sports internship, you might want to be on a sports team or do something else sports-related.

Education: Take Classes

Community colleges and community centers are great places to find out more about a career that interests you, and they're often pretty inexpensive. Look up community colleges in the phone book, and then call them or visit their Web sites to find out about courses.

Volunteer Experience *is* Work Experience

By volunteering, you're helping yourself, but you're also helping your community. If you have a pile of volunteering experience under your belt, you'll not only show that you are a kind-hearted person but you will also impress employers with tons of work experience. Once you apply for a job, your interviewer will take one look at your resume and think, "Wow! What a wonderful person! I'd love to have him/her work here!" (Colleges love volunteers too.) It also gives you another valuable nonfamily-member reference.

Start researching volunteer opportunities in the fields you like. If you want to work in restaurant but can't get a job, volunteer with a soup kitchen. If you want to work with sports and kids, volunteer as a sports coach. (Once you've got experience doing this, you'll have an easier time getting a job as a coach.) For almost any type of a job, there's a corresponding volunteer experience that could help you land a job at a later date.

Experience Makes a Difference

Yeah, it's cool to get paid for your work (and we all need money at some time or another) but sometimes there are opportunities you just can't get paid for. Once you find out what it's like to do stuff that many teens would never get to do—attend editorial meetings in a publishing company, work to build low-cost housing for the homeless, learn to speak three different languages—you'll start to understand what makes interning and volunteering so great. While it may be time consuming, spending the extra effort to seek out work experience can lead to better jobs. It will totally be worth it in the end!

Teen Dream Job

Veterinary Assistant

Sarah O'Neil
17 years old

1. How did you become interested in being a veterinary assistant?
A show called Emergency Vets. *This show was my inspiration. The more I watched it the more I realized that the blood didn't bother me anymore, at least when it came to animals. I began giving actual thought to being a vet.*

2. How did you get your job?
I took my dog in for vaccinations and asked the vet what she suggested I do if I was interested in being a vet. The vet suggested I volunteer and told me I could possibly volunteer at her hospital.

3. How long have you been at your job?
I started volunteering June 2001 and quit volunteering October 2001. I was then hired for a paying position in May 2002.

4. How do you balance work with school and friends?

For the most part you have to be driven. I stay on top of my homework and I only work at the veterinary hospital two days a week. School always comes first before everything, including my friends and my boyfriend. I have to wait until after work to do my homework, but no matter what, I make sure I get it done.

5. What is the hardest part about your job?

The hardest part about my job is memorizing all the information about the vaccines and different procedures we do.

6. What is the best or most rewarding part of your job?

As the doctor says, knowing that we practiced good medicine today. Every day we make an animal's life easier or make them healthier or even save a life. That is the best feeling in the world.

7. What advice would you give to other kids about finding a dream job?

If you know what you want to do, educate yourself about it and go for it. Ask advice from people in the field you're interested in and volunteer. No one turns down a volunteer and you get great experience that way.

8. What is a typical workday like for you?

A typical day is very long. I usually work nine hours a day. For appointments, I take the pulse, respiration, and temperature of the patient and get the history of the patient and what is wrong with them. I also give vaccines, draw blood, and run various blood tests. After the appointments are all over, I clean and close down the hospital. On surgery days I help sedate the animal going into surgery, and then assist in the surgery by monitoring the patient to make sure its pulse, respiration, and temperature are normal. I also help by handing the doctor her instruments and controlling the anesthesia.

CHAPTER 6

You Got the Job!

NOW WHAT?

The phone rings—you're in the middle of taking a shower—and you decide to let the answering machine get it. But then you hear a voice saying, "We'd like to offer you a position." You leap out of the shower and grab the phone just in time. "Hello?" you gasp, praying they haven't hung up yet. "Ms. Green, we'd like to hire you for the cashier position at Amy's Records." "Oh, definitely! That sounds great! When do I start?"

Congratulations! One of the six places you interviewed with has called and offered you the job! But what if that job wasn't your first choice? And, if you receive an offer from your number-one job preference, is it too late to negotiate a better salary? Before you hurry to accept any offer, read this chapter.

Yup, We'd Like to Hire You!

The minute someone offers you a job, don't just accept it. Get any additional details first that were not already covered in the interview. Then ask if you can call him or her back later in the day or the next day.

Before you call them back, be sure you have figured out little things like when you can work, how you're going to get there, and talk to your parents about it. Find out if you can get a ride from your parents or if you'll need to find some other mode of transportation. Once you've figured everything out, call the boss back. Tell him or her that you're eager to work for the company and thank him or her for the opportunity.

Hours

You probably want to know how much you'll have to work (your hours) before you apply, but once you've got the job, go back over it again. Establishing your hours can be really important. Can you work any time from when school ends to your curfew? Or, are there specific times you'll be available to work? Can you only work from 4 PM to 7 PM on Mondays, Wednesdays, and Fridays? Whatever your needs are, be sure to talk to your potential boss about them before you agree to work.

In most states, teenagers under 16 can work only three hours per day, except on weekends. Check your state U.S. Department of Labor or visit www.youthrules.dol.gov/jobs.htm to find out how many hours per day you can work if you're under 16. Your employer should also know this law.

Money!!!

The more experience you have, the more valuable you are to the employer. Your pay will usually reflect your level of experience, so if this is your first job, you may not have a lot of room to negotiate on the pay scale. In the long term, that may be a realistic goal, but in the meantime you may have to be satisfied with minimum wage. Some jobs will pay minimum wage or minimum wage with a discount on products in their store. Still, it never hurts to ask about higher wages and discounts, and it's easier to do this before you're already working. Politeness is the most important part and also

QUIZ: Are You Ready to Work?

1. You get a call for a job offer. You
a) drop the phone on accident and curse loudly.
b) say, "Yes! Yes! I accept! I want to work for you!"
c) say, "That sounds wonderful! May I call you back later today with my decision?"

2. OK, you've been offered the job. But there's another job you're waiting to hear back on, and you'd really rather have that job. So when you call back, you say,
a) "Look, you'll have to wait a while. There's this other job I want more."
b) "Can I have a day or so to let you know my decision?"
c) "I'll take the job!" Why take a chance on having the other job fall through?

3. Uh-oh—you have two job offers, and you want them both! So you
a) call both companies and tell them you want more money—after all, they both want you, right?
b) make a list of pros and cons, then carefully decide which job will be best.
c) panic and take them both.

4. You've made up your mind to take the job, but when you ask about the pay, the employer says minimum wage. You're bummed because you already have two years of experience! After asking for a slight increase, he tells you that the original offer is the best that he can do, so you
a) angrily refuse and tell him you're worth much more than minimum wage.
b) calmly explain that you had hoped for a little more, seeing as you have previous experience.
c) accept minimum wage anyway. Money is money, and you don't want to risk this job.

5. You have everything planned out for your new job, except how to get there. Mom doesn't want to drive you, neither does Dad. You
a) demand that they drive you. You're doing them a favor here—you'll be out of the house!
b) work out a compromise. You'll take the bus from school to work, and then one of them will pick you up from there.
c) decide not to take the job. You've . . . er . . . you've changed your mind.

6. You decided you don't want to take the job after all. It's just not the right fit. So you
a) tell the boss exactly why you don't want to work for his company.
b) tactfully explain you won't be able to accept the position at this time.
c) don't show up on the first day of work.

7. You find out you didn't get the job. So you
a) toilet paper the hiring manager's house the next night.
b) start looking for another job.
c) huddle up at home and cry.

Scoring
1. a=1, b=2, c=3
2. a=1, b=3, c=2
3. a=2, b=3, c=1
4. a=1, b=3, c=2
5. a=1, b=3, c=2
6. a=2, b=3, c=1
7. a=1, b=3, c=2

17–21 points:
You're set! You know how to gracefully accept and decline jobs and should have no problems with future employers.

12–16 points:
You do a good job focusing on your needs and interests, but sometimes small hurdles can get in your way and cause you to overextend yourself. Try to work out the details of the job before you start.

7–11 points:
Remember, you can't have everything you want and there are often undesirable aspects to any job. Try to make wise decisions and to realize that even the most successful people have accepted jobs they weren't thrilled about.

point out the benefits to *the employer* if they have you on board. Mention that with the year of child-care experience you have and your fluent knowledge of Spanish (or whatever your wonderful qualifications are), would they be willing to . . . ?

Work Supplies

Before you start your job, you may have to buy a few work supplies or clothes. You will want to ask about this when they offer you the job so you can go to work your first day fully prepared. Ask your boss what the company policy is on dress codes. If you have to wear a uniform, some companies require that you purchase it (the money to pay for it often comes out of your paycheck).

Other businesses, like restaurants, may require you to wear certain colored shirts, pants, or shoes to work as part of their employee dress policy. If you don't have these items, you'll have to invest the money in purchasing them for your new job. Another important item to get, if you don't have one already, is a watch. Don't go to work without one! With fifteen-minute breaks and half-hour lunches, you want to be sure to get back on time.

Um, Well, See, I Kinda Already Took This Other Job

How to do you—gasp—decline a job? Let's say you applied for two jobs and they both call back, offering to hire you. If you want Job A more, so you accept that job, following the whole procedure: confirming wages, benefits, and hours. What do you do for Job B? Just politely say that you've already accepted another offer. Or if you didn't accept another offer but you've decided you don't want this job, tell the person that you're honored, but you've changed your mind about the job.

Celebrate Your Success!

Hey, don't get too nervous about this. Remember, you got the job! Celebrate! The employer is not going to suddenly change his mind because you asked for fifty cents more every hour. They want to hire you!

Teen Dream Job

Graphic Designer

Jared Cain
16 years old

1. How did you become interested in art?
Art became an interest of mine when I was about four years old or so and I saw my Dad drawing, I asked him if I could also draw, and that's when it all began.

2. How did you start designing logos and CD covers?
I started designing logos last year as one of my art projects for class. I found it fun because I could experiment and use my creativity. I designed a CD cover for my high school band.

3. How did you come up with the idea to sell your art work?
Selling my art work came to me when I drew something and showed it to certain people. One of the people I had shown it to liked it so much that he asked to buy it from me. That was when the idea to sell my work popped into my head.

4. Who helped and encouraged you along the way?
A lot of my help and encouragement came from my teachers but mostly my grandma. She was the one who always gave me drawing tools as presents and always encouraged me to try different art fields.

5. Were you surprised that someone was willing to pay for you artwork?
Yes, I was, and I still am. Some people will pay a good amount for something so small.

6. Describe the time it takes and what process you go through to come up with a design or drawing?
Drawing is something that you have to make a commitment to. It takes a lot of time and practice to do well. When I come up with a design, first I think of what I am drawing and then about things that relate to it. After that, I draw many small thumbnail drawings until I come to a design that suits my fancy.

7. What are the most difficult or stressful things about what you do?
To me, the most difficult and stressful thing is getting the drawing the way you or your customer wants it. Also, it is difficult to get things in on time.

8. What are the most rewarding parts of your job?
The most rewarding thing for me is completing a drawing and then looking at it and getting the feeling that WOW, I can't believe I just drew this, or the happiness that you see in someone's eyes when you give them the drawing the exact way they wanted it.

9. How do you balance school and friends with working on your art projects?
It's easy for me. Art projects take time, and I tell the people who want them how long it might take me to do it. Art is something that you do on your own time. So it easily balances out.

10. What advice would you give to other kids whose dream jobs would be to become artists?
Make sure it's something that you're really interested in because it takes a lot of time and dedication. Also make sure that you have a strong mind and can take criticism well, because in the field of art people deal with that every day. Always put 100% into every drawing, no matter how small it is.

CHAPTER 7

Keeping Work Fun

BOSSES, COWORKERS, AND CUSTOMERS

Your boss takes you around and introduces you to all your coworkers. Within a couple weeks, you are on good terms with many of them—and you're loving your job. It's so much easier to enjoy your work when you enjoy the people there too!

OK, you've got the job, but now you've got to deal with the customers, your coworkers, and of course, your boss. No matter how great of a worker you are and how good your qualifications are, it's important to keep work fun and to learn how to get along with everyone there. Any workplace has a mix of personalities and it can be hard for everyone to get along all the time.

Cool Coworkers

Usually, most coworkers are friendly on the job but you may still come across someone who's difficult to get along with. Here are a few basic suggestions for keeping your work environment positive:

Introduce yourself: First of all, make an effort to meet all your coworkers and to remember their names.

Be friendly: Try to learn more about your coworkers and boss. You'll be surprised about what you'll discover and the friends you might make.

Have good attendance: One of the most important qualities at work is good attendance. Other people are depending on you to show up. If you call in sick at the last minute it can make your boss's and coworkers' jobs tougher. Everyone appreciates someone who is dependable that they can count on.

Follow instructions/rules: When you're new on the job, there are usually plenty of instructions and rules to take in. By making a strong effort to follow these rules, you're showing your boss that you know how to listen and that you're trustworthy enough to accept additional responsibilities.

Be helpful: If you notice that a coworker needs your help, see if you can do anything to make his or her job a little easier. He or she will appreciate the offer and might return the favor.

Avoid talking negatively about your coworkers or boss: Word travels fast, and before you know it, that little comment about your boss's pocket protector could get you into big trouble. Also, you might join a group of coworkers where a feud already exists. Try to make it clear from the beginning that you aren't the one to take sides—especially if the person getting picked on hasn't done anything to you.

Irreconcilable Differences

What happens when you've tried all these things and you still don't get along with your coworkers? Unless there are serious problems, your boss isn't going to fire anyone. So what do you do?

Talk to them: Every once in a while talking can help a bad situation. Say you've noticed that you two don't always get along so well and ask if there's anything you can do to improve the situation. But if "drop dead!" (or something along those lines) is the reply you get, it's time to try another approach.

Be humble: Remember that no one likes a know-it-all. Even if you think you can do a better job than someone else, have respect for the experience of your coworkers.

Change your shift: If talking to the person didn't work, try switching your shift around or working in a different area than him or her, so you don't have to work directly with the problem coworker.

Positive attitude: Wouldn't it be nice if you didn't need to bother with any of these reconciling-differences strategies? There'll always be those infuriating people whom you don't get along with, so try to keep a positive attitude about them if possible.

Ask for help: If nothing else works, talk to your supervisor—not to tattle, but to ask for suggestions on how to fix the situation.

Bad Work Etiquette Scenario

Amelia is new on the job. She spends all her time trying to make her bosses like her but is rude to the secretaries, coworkers, and pretty much everyone else on the job. Though Amelia brings her bosses coffee and donuts, she ignores the secretaries when they say hi to her and barely acknowledges the fact that her coworkers exist.

Good Work Etiquette Scenario

Karolyn is new on the job. She makes an effort to be friendly with everyone. She says hello to each person and remembers everyone's name. Soon all the people begin to notice the new employee who is friendly and nice to everyone.

QUIZ: Bosses, Coworkers, and Customers

1. It's your first day, and your boss is introducing you to everyone. One of your coworkers totally ignores you when you say hello. You
a) politely repeat it. Maybe he didn't hear you.
b) say loudly, "Well, that was rude!"
c) immediately assume that he or she doesn't like you.

2. You're a lifeguard. Your boss asks you to make sure all the pool equipment is put away by 5 PM. At 6 the boss comes and demands to know why everything is still out. You
a) lie and say, "I did put everything away, but some kids got into the shed and scattered it!"
b) apologize and confess that you forgot, but you'll clean it up right away.
c) break down sobbing.

3. One of your friends comes in while you're working the snack counter at the movie theater and begs you to give him some M&Ms, even though he doesn't have any money. You
a) hand him a package of candy and pay for it yourself to keep him from making a scene.
b) yell, "You're interfering with my job! Go get your own job and earn some money to pay for candy, you slacker!"
c) are careful to tell him that he has to pay for the candy just like everyone else.

4. You're promoted over some of your friends at work. You use this new power to
a) try to resolve conflicts, keep people happy, and still make sure the job gets done.
b) help your friends get better hours even if it means messing up other people's schedules.
c) pay them back for that "one time in third grade" by giving them the worst hours possible.

5. Someone is spreading nasty rumors about you at work, and you know exactly who the little weasel is. So you
a) spread nasty rumors back about them. Fight fire with fire, right?
b) privately talk to your boss about the situation and ask if they have any suggestions for how to handle it.
c) become depressed and allow the quality of your work to suffer, leading many people to believe that the rumors are true.

6. You accidently give a customer the wrong change for a twenty. Even though it was unintentional, the customer is extremely rude and angry about the mistake. Your supervisor later informs you to be more careful. You
a) get angry and yell at him, "It wasn't my fault!"
b) calmly apologize and resolve to do better the next time.
c) begin sobbing and go down on your knees, asking for forgiveness.

7. A coworker has told your boss that you made him do a bunch of extra work when it was really the other way around! You
a) allow your boss to lecture you without saying anything.
b) explain to your boss that you and your coworker seem to have very different memories of the event.
c) tell your boss that your coworker is a lying little creep who does nothing but relax while you slave away.

Scoring
1. a=3, b=1, c=2
2. a=1, b=3, c=2
3. a=1, b=2, c=3
4. a=3, b=2, c=1
5. a=1, b=3, c=2
6. a=3, b=2, c=1
7. a=2, b=3, c=1

17–21 points:
You enjoy your job, and get along great with your boss, the customers, and your coworkers—mainly because you make a real effort to be friendly and helpful to the people you come in contact with at work.

12–16 points:
On the job, you make sure things are fair and that you have a good relationship with your coworkers and boss. Sometimes, you may let a rude person get to you, but remember it's not worth all the emotional energy. Try to stay focused on your work

7–11 points:
Remember that you have rights and no job, no matter how much you want to keep it, is worth sacrificing them to please others. If you're really having a tough time, talk your frustrations over with your boss, friend, or a parent.

So who would you rather be, Amelia or Karolyn? Maybe this is a little exaggerated, but part of your job is getting along with the people you work with.

The Customer Is Always Right . . . Well, Sometimes

You've heard it before. "The customer is always right." Yeah, it's clichéd, but it's also true . . . sometimes. The customer is right when he or she isn't happy with a purchased item, or there's been a mistake with his order. The customer is right when you accidentally drop his groceries in the parking lot and break all the eggs.

When is the customer wrong? Good question. The customer is wrong when she is verbally or physically abusive to you. The customer's wrong when he has committed a crime or damaged a piece of property. If you're unsure if the customer you're dealing with is doing something inappropriate, talk to your manager.

Customers may snap at you, make you recount the change, argue with you over what the order really was, or act rude and disrespectful. But they're also paying your salary, so be patient with them.

Bosses: Good, Bad, and Inexcusably Bad

You've probably heard people complain about their boss. They're upset because he won't give them extra vacation time, she won't give them good hours, or he's just an idiot. But many bosses are easy to get along with and try to treat their employees well. In any case, you might as well practice getting along—it's going to be one of the life-long challenges of being in the workforce. Aside from the fact that it'll make your dealings with your boss a lot easier, your boss controls whether or not you keep this job, and he will be the one who decides whether or not to give you a recommendation when this job ends.

Good bosses: Yes, they do exist. In fact, there are many more good bosses out there than bad bosses; you just hear about the bad ones more because people who complain are very loud about it.

Bad bosses: Everyone talks about them. Bad bosses are the kind who criticize your work without telling you how to improve it, make changes in your work schedule without asking you first, or are rude and disrespectful to you. You can deal with a bad boss the same way you deal with a bad customer or coworker: be patient. Try to understand where he or she is coming from. If you can't understand, even after trying to look at the situation from every possible angle, or if you can tell that what they're doing is legally wrong, look at the next category.

Inexcusably bad bosses: These bosses may take action that's illegal, harassing, or discriminating. They may treat you differently because of their prejudices or be friendly with you in a way that's inappropriate. What's your best bet for getting out of that kind of situation? You can try talking to your boss or another manager you feel comfortable with. If they don't listen to you though or if you feel uncomfortable talking to them about it, go to your parents. You might want to ask them about leaving the job, or talking to your boss's supervisor.

Patience Is the Key

There's one overwhelming rule when it comes to dealing with other people on the job. Be patient. Be patient with your coworker when he can't figure out where to unload the shipment of mustard. Be patient with your boss when he changes your schedule for the fifth time that month. Be patient with the customers when they fumble around for those expired coupons. In the end, it all pays off. Literally.

Teen Dream Job

Professional Chocolate Makers

Elise and Evan Macmillan
15 and 18 years old

1. How did you become interested in making chocolate?

Elise: *I first started making candies with my grandmother. I have always liked chocolate and creating new things. Together, Evan and I came up with the idea to sell handmade, farm-inspired chocolates.*

Evan: *When we were thinking about a product to sell, the market for chocolate seemed like a good one because it is a large and growing market. Chocolate is a product people love and they always seem to want more of. Chocolate-making is a happy business!*

2. How much help did you have in setting up your business and from whom?

Elise & Evan: *We have had the help of many support groups to nurture our venture from a "kid's" business to what we are today. While we relied on the encouragement and support of family and friends, we also looked to experts in institutions and organizations for advice and direction. Long before we started the Chocolate Farm (www.chocolatefarm.com), we became involved with the Young Americans Bank, now part of the Young Americans' Center for Financial Education. They provided us with our first formal education in personal finance, global economics, and entrepreneurship. They sponsored the Holiday Marketplace where we first sold our chocolates, gave us our first business loan, and are now loyal customers of the Chocolate Farm.*

3. What is the most rewarding part of your job?
Elise: *Hearing from people all over the world (young and old) who have been inspired by our business adventure.*
Evan: *It has been an opportunity of a lifetime to learn in a very hands-on way about business, economics, and people.*

4. What is the most difficult part of your job?
Elise: *Finding time to do everything I want to do.*
Evan: *Keeping up with the rapid growth of the business.*

5. How do you balance spending time with friends and doing schoolwork with your job?
Elise & Evan: *Our obligations to family and school take priority over obligations to our business. We also reserve time for friends, athletics, music, and just being kids. We try to schedule our time so that business meetings, phone calls, and answering e-mail work around our other commitments. We also have a group of employees who make it possible for us to do well at school, while having a fun and successful business.*

6. What advice would you give to other kids searching for their dream jobs?
Elise & Evan: *Our advice to teenagers thinking of starting a business is to find something they love to do, learn all they can about it, and share it with others. Share your resources and help your community. Above all, enjoy the ride. By the time your peers have graduated from college, you could have five or ten years of informal business training under your belt.*

7. What's the most important life lesson you have learned?
One important life lesson we have learned is that a successful business is based on trust and that the business has to earn that trust. One of the early obstacles in beginning our business was our lack of a track record. It was not unusual for a customer or supplier early on to ask, "Can I speak with your parents?" At ages 10 and 13 we were asking customers and suppliers to put their trust in us and we had to earn their trust over time by creating good products and delivering on our promises.

CHAPTER 8

Your Job and the Law

DECIPHERING THE LEGAL JARGON

You're 15. It's 11 PM, you're still at work, and you have your English final tomorrow. Your boss has scheduled you to close up—that means working until midnight. When you get home, you'll have to study all night, and you'll get maybe an hour of sleep. Sound good? Wait a minute. Is this really legal? Is a fifteen-year-old really allowed to stay out until midnight working? Nope. There's little things called labor laws that keep your boss from making you work late. So go home, enjoy your sleep, and thank the U.S. government.

Labor laws may not seem important, but they're what guarantee you get paid a decent wage, have breaks, and get lunch. In this chapter, find out about the different laws that affect you, your pay, and your working conditions, as well as the rights you have on the job.

How Old Do You Have to be to Work Legally?

If you're not in high school yet (meaning if you're under 14), your options are somewhat restricted because of child labor laws. But there are plenty of really fun, interesting jobs for kids thirteen and younger out there. Here are a few:

You can start your own business: It can pay really well and you get to be your own boss if you do it right, which means not getting stuck working early Saturday mornings. You can offer to babysit, mow lawns, take care of people's animals while there away, etc.

Work one of the following jobs: You can act, work on a farm (only in non-hazardous jobs), deliver newspapers, or work in a business owned solely by one of your parents (parental permission or special work permits may be required for some of these jobs). You're not covered by minimum wage rules if you're under twelve. And in order to do farm work, it has to be certified as nonhazardous by the U.S. Department of Labor. Check out its Web site for teens, youthrules.dol.gov, to find out more.

If You're 14 or 15

On a school day, and if you can really manage to squeeze your job in between basketball practice, school newspaper meetings, and homework, you can work 3 hours a day. But those 3 hours have to happen between 7 AM and 7 PM (meaning not having to get up really early to go to work, or working until midnight when you should be finishing your homework). And you can't work during school hours (meaning that even if you've got a couple free periods, you're out of luck). You're permitted to work 18 hours each week during the school year.

You've got a little bit more freedom when it comes to days without any school—weekends, summer breaks, and holidays. On non-school days, the U.S. Department of Labor will let you work 8 hours per day and as late as 9 PM. You can also work a maximum of 40 hours per week in the summer. For those over 16, there is no limit to the amount of hours you can work during the summer. Now, I don't recommend doing this, since you'll probably need more than two days a week to relax, but it's nice to know you've got room to expand.

Working Conditions

There are some nice rules about working conditions and things like breaks. You get a rest period of at least 15 minutes for every 4 hours you work and at least a half-hour meal period no later than 5 hours and a minute after you come to work (the labor laws are very specific when it comes to food). Also, your boss can't force you to try to lift a weight that's too heavy for you.

By law, employers must provide a safe workplace employees by complying with federal occupational safety and health standards. Some of these standards include providing protective gear and equipment for employees, and training employees to make them aware of safety hazards. If there is a job you feel uncomfortable doing for safety reasons, before you start anything, talk to your supervisor and make sure you are old enough to do the work, and have the proper safety gear and training. If you're still unsure whether your working environment is safe, talk to your parents or visit the Web site www.osha.gov for more information.

Your Right to Money

Ah, the big one. You have to be paid minimum wage, which is (at the time this book was written) $5.15 per hour. There are some exceptions to this minimum wage. In many states, jobs where you receive tips can pay you less than the federal minimum wage because they count your tips toward your total wage. Also, remember that $5.15 is the Federal minimum wage; a lot of states have a higher minimum wage. For the first 90 days you work, your employer can pay you less than minimum wage, but no less than $4.25 per hour. This rule applies to people under 20, and is regarded by many employers as a training wage. There are lots of jobs for teens that pay more than $4.25 per hour. For example, a typical lifeguard job might pay $8 per hour. Not bad, eh?

QUIZ: Find Out How Much You Know About Labor Laws

1. During your interview, the interviewer asks if you are religious. You
a) are offended and declare "That's none of your business!"
b) are so shocked that you just sit there in stunned silence.
c) say calmly, "My religious beliefs have no bearing on how well I can do this job."

2. You're fifteen and you apply for a job at a deli. You're offered the job, and they tell you you'll be making sandwiches in the back room. You
a) accept. Why wouldn't you?
b) decline. You know the law: if you're under 16, you have to make the food in front of the customers, not in a back room. It's Federal law.
c) asks if there's a different position available, where you can work at the front counter.

3. It's 8:30 at night in the summer, and you're ready to go home. The café stays open till 11. Suddenly your 22-year-old coworker begs you to stay and close up late—his girlfriend has tickets to a concert at 10, and he has to leave now. You say
a) "Sorry, buddy. You signed up for this shift. Guess the concert will have to wait."
b) "I wish I could, but because I'm under 16, legally I can't work past 9."
c) "Oh . . . um, OK, I guess."

4. Your mom thinks you can only work 18 hours during a school week, since you're not 16 yet. You inform her that
a) um, well, you think it might be only 10.
b) there is no limit on how many hours you can work! That would be unfair!
c) she's right, and you're glad she's taken the time to look it up.

5. To use machinery like a forklift when you're working, you have to be
a) eighteen.
b) fourteen.
c) insane.

6. If an employer discriminates against you because you're a teenager, you
a) blink in surprise. Employers discriminate against teens?
b) do nothing. Age discrimination laws only apply if you're over 18.
c) sue.

7. You're 15 and decide to apply for a job as a forest firefighter, until you realize
a) the smoke may not be great for your asthma.
b) you have to be at least 16 to help fight forest fires.
c) your parents would kill you if they found out you were doing such a dangerous job.

Scoring
1. a=1, b=2, c=3
2. a=1, b=2, c=3
3. a=2, b=3, c=1
4. a=2, b=1, c=3
5. a=3, b=2, c=1
6. a=2, b=3, c=1
7. a=1, b=3, c=2

17–21 points:
Nice! Someone who knows something about law. You do a good job standing up for your rights without being too confrontational. Keep it up!

12–16 points:
Remember to stay informed, know your legal rights, and speak up for yourself! Sometimes it can be a pain keeping current on labor laws, but the alternative is that you may run the risk of letting people walk all over you.

7–11 points:
No one tramples your rights. Just be careful with your approach and be sure your legal defense isn't unnecessarily offensive to others. Remember, these laws apply to other people, too.

Hazardous Jobs

If you're under 18, there are some jobs that are against the law for you to do. (Disclaimer: these are NOT all of the jobs declared hazardous by the U.S. Department of Labor. Before you accept a job, check to make sure it's legal for you to do it).

If You're Too Young to Drive, You're Too Young for . . .

◆ construction work (that means painting, repair, demolition . . . everything having to do with construction).

◆ fighting fires or clearing land (includes operating a tractor).

◆ working one of those rides at amusement parks.

◆ handling certain chemicals, like dry fertilizer or insecticides.

If You're Too Young to Vote, You're Too Young to . . .

◆ make or store things that blow up. (You know, bombs.)

◆ drive a vehicle. (Under limited circumstances, you can do this if you're 17.)

◆ mine.

◆ work in a sawmill.

◆ use power-driven tools.

◆ work in a place where you're exposed to stuff that might turn you into a superhero (i.e., radioactive material).

◆ slaughter or meat-pack.

◆ make bricks or tiles.

◆ use a wrecking ball, dynamite, anything like that (i.e., demolition).

◆ put a roof on somebody's house.

Discrimination

Most of the same discrimination laws apply to teens, but not all of them. There are no laws to protect teenagers from age discrimination (or "ageism," if you prefer). But it's still totally illegal for anyone to discriminate against you because of your sex, your religion, or your ethnic background.

So There You Are

Those are your rights—remember them! Photocopy them from this book and keep them handy. Most employers are great, and they won't try to violate your rights. These laws are just here to help you be happy and safe on the job.

Teen Dream Job

Runway Model

Elise Hoyt
16 years old

1. How did you become interested in modeling?
I think most of my life, I thought about being a model in the back of my mind, but never seriously. Several people told me I should think about pursuing it. Last summer, I was at the county fair, my sister was involved in 4-H and I was helping her. John Casablanca's (a modeling agency) had a booth at the fair and said that I had the "look."

2. What did you do to prepare to become a model?
After I signed up with John Casablanca's, I had to go to school for several months to learn how to walk down the runway, make the right turns, and apply makeup. No one in my family wears makeup, so it was all pretty new to me. It was fun—I really had a blast. I have a friend who models in New York, and he gave me a book that helped me prepare for the classes at John Casablanca's.

3. What does your job consist of?

I've been asked to model prom dresses and bridal gowns. I also have to do photo shoots with a recruiter. Some of my photos are sent to movies, commercials, and other modeling agencies across the country.

4. What is the most challenging part of what you do?

Modeling is a hard business because you get rejected. There is also a chance that someone may ask you to model something you don't feel comfortable wearing. So far I've been blessed that all the people I work with respect my values. It's really important for teens to know that you have to be who you are, not what the business wants to make you. It's a job where you really have to know yourself.

6. How do you balance school with modeling?

School and grades are very important to me. Even though I love modeling, I would never let it get in the way my other goals. On the way to a modeling job, I often bring my homework in the car with me.

7. What advice would you give to other kids who are searching for their dream jobs?

Always try new things; you never know where you will succeed. Once you've found something you like, if you can apply yourself, you can go extremely far in life.

8. What do you find most rewarding about modeling?

I find modeling extremely fun. The people you meet are interesting and it's been a whole new experience. I've discovered more about myself. I've learned that if I work hard at this job, I can do well at it.

CHAPTER 9

On the Road Again

LEAVING YOUR JOB

The summer is over—sob—and you're about to begin your junior year. You've bought your car, and there's no chance you can manage to keep working. How do you leave without making your boss upset with you?

Most of the time, you leave your job by choice. School's starting and you can't handle work too, you've found a better job, you're not enjoying your job anymore, or you just don't want to keep working—maybe it's too much strain in your life or it cuts into your free time. Every once in a while, you may get fired, but that's usually if you do something like stealing, not showing up for work, or repeatedly arriving to work late. Sometimes you have to leave the company because it is downsizing and laying off workers. This chapter is about the different reasons for leaving your job—whether you are planning to or not—and how to do it *tactfully*.

QUIZ: Are You Ready to Leave Your Job?

1. You're thinking about leaving your job because you have to go back to school, but you want to test the waters and see how receptive the boss will be about your return next year. You
a) talk loudly about what you plan to do next year whenever your boss is in hearing distance, hoping she'll take the hint and ask you to come back.
b) mention to your boss that you'd like to come back next summer once school ends and see how she reacts.
c) ask your friend to ask the boss to rehire you next year.

2. You know your performance hasn't been so great lately—you've been late on several occasions and haven't called first to let your boss know—but it's because your teachers have gone insane with homework. What do you do?
a) Moan about the horrible amount of homework you have and continue arriving late to work.
b) Talk to your boss and explain to her what's going on. She may not be happy with you, but at least she may be sympathetic.
c) Make an extra effort to call next time and let your boss know that you're coming in late.

3. You're sick of your job—the hours are long, the pay is awful, and you don't get along with anyone there. How do you tell the boss?
a) Completely slack off until the boss fires you.
b) Politely let him know that you're giving your two weeks notice.
c) Explain that your last day of work will be Friday (even though today is Tuesday).

4. You're ready to quit, but you could really use a reference from this boss. When you quit, you say,
a) "So long, loser! I'm sick of this job, and I'm out of here!"
b) "Here's my two weeks' notice."
c) "As much as I've enjoyed working here, I'm afraid it's become necessary for me to move on. Please consider this my two weeks' notice."

5. Your boss had to fire you for arriving to work late. You
a) start screaming curses at him and storm out.
b) nod and exit.
c) say, "I'm sorry it didn't work out. Thanks again for giving me this opportunity." Then leave.

6. You have to quit your summer job because you're going back to school. So to end your relationship with the company, you

a) start inexplicably missing work and then calling in a few days later with a lame excuse.

b) explain that school is starting, so you won't be able to continue working, but you are sure to mention that you really enjoyed working with them.

c) totally relax and slack off. You don't need this job anymore, so why not do what you want?

7. You really would like to find another job, so you:

a) put in your two weeks notice and don't look for another job until you're out of money.

b) you decide to look around for a better job first, then put in your two weeks notice once you've found one.

c) quit.

SCORING

1. a=2, b=3, c=1
2. a=1, b=3, c=2
3. a=1, b=3, c=2
4. a= 1, b= 2, c=3
5. a= 1, b= 2, c=3
6. a= 1, b= 3, c=2
7. a= 2, b= 3, c=1

17–21 points: You have a good idea of how to deal with your boss (and how to deal with leaving your job). You're set!

12–16 points: Everyone's afraid of talking to his or her boss. Practice with your friends and be sure you know what you want to say and you'll do fine.

7–11 points: Being direct is the best approach, so don't rely on dropping hints hoping to resolve problems. Your boss may not be happy to hear that you're leaving, but she or he will respect your decision.

School Bells Ringing

Let's talk about the happiest of these possibilities first: school is starting, and you can't keep working. Maybe your parents have told you that under no circumstances can you work during the school year; maybe you've realized that there's so much you have to do for school, it's impossible to also work. The beginning of school is a really inconvenient time to stop working, because you need money the most during school, for relaxing with friends, seeing movies, buying almost anything you can get your hands on . . . the list goes on forever.

Before you give notice make sure your boss knows that you liked your job and are only leaving because you have to return to school. In fact, it doesn't hurt to ask about getting your job back once school ends, since, if they say yes, you have a nearly-guaranteed job offer for next summer. It's also important to give your boss plenty of time (a minimum of two weeks is best) to find someone to replace you.

How do you talk to your boss? There are several different ways. Number one is probably the simplest: "I'll be starting school in a month; please consider this my two weeks' notice. Thanks for giving me the chance to work here." Try to find a time when your boss is not really busy and you can talk to him or her alone. Number two is for situations when telling your boss is only a formality, because your job had a set duration: "Since my time here will be ending in two weeks, I want to thank you for all the help you've given me and everything you've taught me while I've been here."

You've Found a New Job

Your best bet when it comes to leaving one job for another is to be honest with your boss from the beginning. Tell your boss that you're leaving because you've had another job offer and then mention where you're going. Your boss may wish you well or might offer you a raise to keep you there.

Why are you leaving, come to think of it? Do you want a higher salary? A more interesting job? A job that'll be a resume-booster? You'd better have it figured out before you leave, because job-hopping, switching from one job to another in a short period of time, does not cause prospective employ-

ers to line up at your door, begging you to work for them. Think about it—
do you have to leave your job, or could you make it better by staying for a
little longer and working through the problems? Well, consider it. And if
not, be honest with your boss.

Try this: "I wanted to give you my two weeks' notice. I really like working here but decided to accept a job at another company because (better
hours, higher pay, closer to home, all of the above)." Simple, right? Until
you say it, anyway. If you're not a confident person, practice; if you are, go
ahead and say it.

Quitting

You just want to quit. You've tried your best, but you can't take it anymore.
This is the time to really evaluate your situation. Do you really need the
income? Do you have another job lined up? The main problem with quitting your job and not having another place to go (aside from the fact that
you lose that income) is that it looks really bad on your resume. Future
employers are looking for committed employees. Think long term. If you
don't have another job lined up, consider staying until you have a lead on a
new job. For example, what if you quit only to find out later that nobody
else is hiring?

But if you're desperate to leave, go. Even if you despise everything about
your job, you still want to get a good reference. Try this: "I want you to
know that I'm quitting for personal reasons. Please consider this my two
weeks' notice." Isn't that better than "You know what? I hate you. I hate this
job. I hate everything about this place. So I QUIT!"? Seems like it to me.
(And remember, don't complain about a bad job at your next interview; just
use the experience to help you make a better choice next time.)

Getting Fired

Yeah, it stinks. It can be the worst kind of rejection. So how do you deal
with being fired? Buy a lot of chocolate with your remaining salary and get
to work revising your resume. You'll have to be pretty careful in your next
interview when you explain why you left this job. Think up a good diplo-

matic euphemism for "I was fired," such as "it was time to move on" or something like that. If you're delicate about it, hopefully the interviewer will understand what happened.

Moving On

Leaving a job is tough, it's true, but at least you have something to add to your resume. If you're lucky, you can do it without causing too much trouble—and maybe even get a reference out of it! Remember that no one expects you to stay in one job forever. You might want to try out different jobs throughout high school to find out what fits you best, rather than stick with the first one you get.

Teen Dream Job

Entrepreneur and Beekeeper

Jon Eischen
16 years old

1. How did you get your job?
When I was 13 years old, my sister and I were selling flowers from our farm at a local farmer's market. At the market, I met a guy who sold honey sticks, this gave me an idea. We had honeybees on our farm, so I started thinking we could sell honey as well as the flowers. My grandmother and I had the idea that we could use my grandfather's plums to make a special plum-flavored honey.

2. How did you come up with the recipe for plum honey?
I experimented with different combinations of honey and plums. Then I had the whole family try the different samples until everyone agreed on the best one. Now we have three different types of gourmet honey: PlumHoney™, CranHoney™, and PassionHoney™.

3. Did people have a hard time taking a 13-year-old seriously?
Business people really give me leeway when I'm doing my presentations about Little Oak Farms. They see that I'm a kid and they don't give me a hard time. They usual give me lots of good advice because they want to encourage kids like me.

4. What is the most difficult part of your job?

Missing out on the Friday night football game with my friends can be tough. Often, I'll have to prep Friday nights for selling at the farmer's market on Saturday. However my friends also work with me at my booth to help sell our honey.

5. What is the most rewarding part of your job?

It's cool to see a product that you're part of and helped to create. And of course there's the extra money to spend.

6. What were some challenging experiences that you had to deal with?

I used to print our labels on my grandmother's printer. One time I was selling honey outside and it started raining and all the ink on the labels started washing away. It was discouraging but I didn't give up. I learned about printing methods and found glossy labels that you could print on and that wouldn't smear in the rain. I learned that you should never give up when you come to a problem and never be afraid to try a new idea.

7. What's it like working as a beekeeper?

As a beekeeper, I have to maintain and closely watch all the hives. If a specific hive starts to lose bees or the queen bee, I can help by adding a few new bees, feeding honey to them or supplying a new queen bee to bring the hive back to good health. I also wear protective clothing, though sometimes a bee or two will find a way to sneak in—ouch! It takes me about 5 to 10 minutes to get into the protective clothing. When I take it off I'm watching for bees that could still be on my suit, so sometimes it takes a little longer to get out of it.

www.LittleOakFarms.com

Dream Jobs You Can Get RIGHT NOW!

CHAPTER 10

The Write Stuff

NEWS REPORTING AND OTHER WRITING JOBS

Love to write? Maybe you spend all your free time creating stories or your last school paper was five pages over the limit. Now imagine getting paid for all that writing you do—just by telling stories or writing opinion pieces or letting everyone know the best ways to do something—by book, newspaper, or magazine.

The Life of a Writer

There are several jobs that pay when it comes to writing, and some that don't but still make it worth your while. And of course there are those hidden benefits of some writing jobs, such as setting your own hours (that means sleeping in) and being your own boss. There are also some benefits to volunteering or interning in writing-related jobs. For example, internships with a publishing company can show you what an author does to get published. (In fact, my internship with Beyond Words Publishing led me to publishing this book.)

Teen Jobs for the Writer in You

Reporter: A reporter or journalist gathers the news and shares it with the public. If you work for a newspaper, editors send you on assignments to cover an event—maybe a break-in at the neighborhood market, someone famous coming to your town, or a teenager who's broken a record. Contact your local newspapers to see if they use student reporters. If they don't, pull together some examples of your best writing and suggest that they give you a try.

Reviewer: Have you ever daydreamed about getting paid to watch movies, read books, play video games, listen to music, or eat great food? Or have you ever seen reviews in the paper or on the Internet and wondered who gets to do that? Becoming a reviewer is pretty straightforward: Rent, buy, or check out some recent books, movies, or video games (whatever interests you most) and then write up some reviews. You may want to first look at some reviews by other people to see what kinds of structures different publications use. Then submit your reviews to a newspaper, magazine, or Web site with a cover letter asking if they would be interested in having you write more reviews for them. Just as an example, the magazine *Stone Soup* pays $30 per book review and will send books to you (although you don't get to keep them). A big downside of reviewing, though, is that you'll most likely end up as a freelancer, which means you don't work for a company but must compete with other freelance reviewers for each assignment rather than getting paid a steady wage.

Author: Are you constantly writing story ideas on scratch paper? Maybe becoming an author is for you. Writing allows people to explore many kinds of literature, from fiction to poetry. If you are passionate about your writing and send it to the right publisher, you can be paid for writing about what you love. Some successful teen authors include Amelia Atwater-Rhodes and Mattie J. Stepanek. Amelia Atwater-Rhodes was published when she was only 14, and Mattie J. Stepanek got his first book, *Heartsongs*, published when he was 11. His books have made it onto the *New York Times*

Best-Seller List—something that only a tiny percentage of authors will ever achieve. If you decide on a career as an author, there are lots of great books to help you get published. *So, You Wanna be a Writer?* by Cathleen Greenwood and Vicki Hambleton is a good one. But the basic steps are simple: after lots of writing, editing, and researching what company would be the best to publish your manuscript, you send your writing to the publisher. Anywhere from one week to six months later, the publisher will tell you whether or not it wants to publish your work.

Bookstore customer service: Working at a bookstore can give you lots of exposure to new books and even a chance to meet authors at book signings. Meeting authors means one more person you know in the publishing world who's on your side. Some authors are willing to read your writing and recommend it to their publisher or agent; others will edit your work for you. Even if they don't have time to read your work, published authors can be great mentors and can give you advice on getting published. Working at a bookstore gives you exposure to new books, for one, and if you love to write, you probably love to read. As a staff member, you could get a discount. Who wouldn't want that? Plus, reading new books means you'll see lots of different writing styles, and those styles will show in your writing. You'll also see what sells and what doesn't—which is essential information for people who want to get published or who want to keep working in the book-selling world.

Editor: Though you might not realize it, lots of teens have the power to work as editors and help shape what you read. Some teens edit books through publishing companies, while others work for magazines, editing the articles you love to read each month. If you check out an internship directory from the library, it'll give you the contact information for almost any publishing company or magazine that you want to work for, and you can use that information to find out about jobs with any company. So much of publishing is done over the Internet or by e-mail that you don't necessarily have to live near a magazine or book publisher to work for them. Your library's directories, such as the *Literary Marketplace* and *Writer's Market* for book publishing, can show you what is in your area.

Tutoring and teaching: There are plenty of opportunities to get paid while teaching other kids about writing or reading. Parents whose children are having trouble in school are always eager to hire a student with good grades to help their kids learn. Ask your parents if their friends' kids need any help or advertise your tutoring services through your local community center. Many elementary, middle, and high schools also offer student tutoring programs and pay the tutors.

Activities That Can Help You Get the Job

School newspapers: Do you like the idea of seeing your headline across the front page and your name underneath? Then start your own newspaper or join the school newspaper as a reporter. This is one of the best things you can do to help your career as a writer. You'll learn about what goes into producing a newspaper and help perfect a more professional writing style.

School literary magazines: If you're not into intrepid-reporter stuff and you'd rather write fiction and poetry, try your school's literary magazine. These are usually a collection of students' poetry, stories, and essays, printed and bound. These groups are always understaffed, so you might be able to do a lot more on a lit magazine than you would on a newspaper. If the school doesn't have one, start one! Write a proposal that explains what would be in your literary magazine, and then submit your proposal to whoever controls the funding for new clubs, such as the student government or the principal. Talk to your English teachers about strong writers in different grades to drum up some interest from other kids who like to write.

Libraries: Try volunteering at your local library. You may not make money but some libraries will give you hold priority (in other words, if there are ten holds on a book, yours is always first) and sometimes waive fines. If you take out enough books, this can be even better than getting paid. The benefits of a library jobs are a lot like the benefits of working at a bookstore: many libraries hold readings, where you'll get a chance to meet authors, you will be around other people who like words, and plus, there are all those books.

Internships: Wanna know what it's like on the editor's side of the desk? Intern at a publishing company. You'll get a chance to read book submissions, attend editorial meetings, and edit books! You could even find yourself with a book contract. Or you might find that you like writing about books more than writing them yourself, which could set you on a path of writing press releases or copy for catalogs and book jackets. You could also intern for magazines and newspapers and learn about the excitement of getting news out fast or doing research for a big story.

CHAPTER 11

The Great Outdoors

EXPLORING NATURE

You love to be outside, roaming around and looking at all the cool things that surround you. Bugs don't scare you and you're fascinated by plants and animals. If you prefer spending your time outside in the sunshine rather than inside filing papers, working outdoors might be for you.

Outdoor Life

The outdoors is a great place to stretch your legs, breathe fresh air, and explore, so what could be better than getting paid to be out there? Life outside is always different; with our rapidly changing world there's always something new to discover. You can enjoy this benefit while you earn money or gain experience showing others how to enjoy nature or work to conserve and protect the environment.

Teen Jobs for the Outdoors Lover in You

Lifeguard: Die-hard *Baywatch* fan? Find out what it's really like to be a lifeguard. And who knows, you could end up with some hot lifeguard friends. Lifeguarding isn't just about rescuing a drowning swimmer; lifeguards also teach people about water safety and provide first aid for all kinds of injuries. Along with patrolling the waters at a pool, lake, or ocean, lifeguards give lessons in everything from CPR to swimming. You'll have to take a number of safety tests to become a certified lifeguard.

Camp counselor: Do you dream of sleeping under the stars or leading a wilderness hike? Camp counselors get to share their love of nature with others. They become role models for their campers and teach them facts about wildlife. You could choose to work at an overnight camp or a day camp. If you're musical, you can be a counselor at a music camp; if you're into science, there are countless science camps; if you like the arts, believe me, you won't have any trouble finding an art camp that needs counselors. Most religions also hold some sort of camp or youth retreat, and public park services often have many kinds of day camps.

Farm work: If you don't live on a farm you may not realize the opportunities open to you. Many farms take on extra help in the harvest seasons—and lots of cities and towns have small farms right on the outskirts. Picking berries or helping to bale hay is a great way to enjoy the outdoors. Get involved in farming, enjoy the outdoors, and see food production firsthand.

Landscaping assistant: Do you get excited about the flower beds in your front yard? Maybe you should consider landscaping. This job lets you do everything from mowing lawns and sculpting hedges to designing a backyard paradise. Start by contacting your neighbors or a local landscaping company to see if they need any help.

Activities That Can Help You Get the Job

Volunteer with parks and recreation services, zoos, or aquariums:
Volunteers at federal, state, and city parks work hard to keep trails useable
and safe, public gardens weed-free and watered, and garbage in its place. You
can help them keep nature beautiful and enjoyable for future generations.
Volunteers at zoos and aquariums help with nature classes and tours. And
when they have a paid position open, these big organizations often prefer to
hire a volunteer who already knows how things are run.

Start a club: Want to lead nature hikes and river-rafting excursions? Get
some friends together and begin an outdoor pursuits club. Try rock-
climbing, hiking, white-water rafting . . . anything active and outside! If
your dream outdoors job is one of these things that you like to do but
haven't done very often, this is a good way to get more experience (and to see
if you'd really like it).

Learn CPR and first aid: Many jobs, like lifeguarding or being a camp
counselor, require safety knowledge, including CPR and other forms of first
aid. The best place to find courses is the American Red Cross (www.red
cross.org). This organization has all kinds of courses you can take, and when
you complete a course you receive a certificate that can help you get the job.

Join 4-H or FFA: These clubs give teens practical training and experience in
a number of farming and domestic fields. While 4-H (which stands for
Head, Heart, Hands, and Health) sponsors indoor activities, it, like FFA
(Future Farmers of America), also gives kids the opportunity to raise animals, judge produce and livestock, and enjoy the outdoors. Contact either of
these Web sites for more information: www.4-h.org or www.ffa.org.

CHAPTER 12

Music

FROM JEWEL TO JIMMY EAT WORLD

You haven't taken your headphones off since you bought them in the third grade. You can't take a shower without belting out a few songs, and your CD collection won't even fit in your room anymore. Do you know—or want to know—everything about every band on the planet? If music is in your blood, why not let that guide you to a music-related job?

The Life of a Musician

Finally, those lessons have paid off! You might sing or play instruments and if you're lucky, you'll get discovered, have a number-one CD, and make music without having to take a day job to support yourself. Of course, that's the big dream (and it is possible for some lucky kids). But there are many, many other jobs that are fun and exciting, without necessarily making you a household name. Whether you prefer punk, rap, classical, or country, you can find a job that's related to the music you like.

Teen Jobs for the Music Lover in You

Radio DJ: Visit your local community radio station to see what it would take to start your own show or to work as an intern or assistant. You would have the opportunity to play and present your favorite musicians and songs to the listening public. As a radio DJ, you would get to interview guests on the air, as well as answer calls from your listeners. Or you might get to intern for or assist a DJ at the radio station. Look in the phone book; the radio stations will be listed there.

Musician: You can perform at coffee shops or small restaurants. Sometimes these places will take a cover charge from their customers or let you sell your own CDs. Or you can set up a tip jar and customers can give money to your band if they feel like it. Even without making the big bucks, performance experience is essential for anyone who really wants to be a professional musician, and getting out there lets people know about you and your band. Who knows? Maybe you'll get some fans!

Music supply store customer service: How do you like the idea of being surrounded by huge, expensive drum sets, gorgeous electric guitars, and piles of sheet music? Get a job at a music supply store and your dream will come true. You may also get discounts on instruments and equipment (and their repair and maintenance), accessories, and lessons. You'll also be working around other people who love music and who probably work as musicians part time. They may give you tips on playing or getting gigs.

CD shop customer service: If you love your CD collection, this is the place for you. Hey, think of the employee discount. Ten percent (a typical discount) is a lot when you're buying $15 CDs. Sometimes stores even do promotional events with musicians and radio stations, but even if your store doesn't, you'll love getting to hear everything new right when it comes out.

Concert hall attendant: Feel like listening to Mozart, Vivaldi, and Bach every day as you take tickets and usher people to their seats? Get a job at a concert hall and you'll usually get to attend the performances for free.

Concert concessions: This may not be the most glamorous job, but if you want to be closer to seeing plenty of bands play and you can't afford the tickets, you can work at a concession stand at a concert venue. You might find out more about the way things work backstage, how concerts get promoted, or perhaps even catch sight of your favorite singer up close!

Give music lessons: Know a kid in your neighborhood whose violin playing could wake the dead? If you have a lot of experience playing a musical instrument, offer to be his music teacher. You can also advertise your teaching services through a music supply store or at your school. Private instructors can make a lot of money per hour, but they only work a few hours each week.

Sound crew: Do you want to play an active role in the production of music? A sound crew works as a team to present the best music to the audience. With this job you might record, balance music levels, help avoid amp feedback, and edit the music and voice with different kinds of equipment. You may not be in the limelight, but you are a large part of the success that results!

Activities That Can Help You Get the Job

Your own band: If you love music but you're not so enthusiastic about standing on a stage alone, find some friends and start a band. You'll get to hang out with your friends and play music. You can do covers, perform your own music, or both. Working in a band is great for honing your performance skills and if you plan to be in a band in the future, it's good to learn how to work as a group. Plus, your garage band could be the next to go big and sign a multimillion dollar contract!

Choir: Not into instruments? Join your local community, school, or church choir. Singing in a group is one more way to learn from the experts—those in the choir with you and the one directing up front. It will also help you work out all those butterflies before you start soloing at Carnegie Hall.

School band: Join the school band to keep developing your skills. You'll get good exposure (especially if you're in high school; some bands go all over the country or even the world) and the chance to hang out with lots of other musically oriented people at your school.

Youth orchestra: Audition for a youth orchestra. You may not get paid, but it's one of the best ways to gain experience performing. Plus, the biggest youth orchestras travel around the country and give concerts. Some colleges offer scholarships to strong musicians with this kind of experience.

Internships: Have you daydreamed about having a studio produce your own CD? Intern with a recording studio to find out exactly how they do it. And don't forget, that supervisor of yours will still be looking for musicians when your band gets its act together.

Promote your favorite band: Are you lucky enough to know a great musician or band? Ask to help promote their next show. Post signs or pass out flyers for the band in exchange for help and advice from the musicians. See if one of them will be your mentor. Just don't be surprised if you end up sitting with the roadies at concerts.

CHAPTER 13

Entertainment

ACTING, RADIO, TV, AND MORE!

Do you like to make people laugh? Can you do impressions that even Jim Carrey would be proud of? Ever picture yourself smiling on a forty-foot screen while hordes of people stare at you and eat overpriced popcorn and candy? You might be a natural for acting on stage, on TV, or in movies.

Life as an Actor

Not all actors live in Hollywood. They can live all over the world and work in stage productions, in commercials, on TV, or in the movies. Acting gives people the chance to try on different personas and to escape into a fictional world with a script, sets, and costumes. The beauty of acting lies in its versatility: while you might begin a career on stage, you could move into commercials and movies and eventually decide to try directing or producing. People like Tom Hanks, Robert Redford, and many others both act and direct.

Teen Jobs for the Actor in You

Stage: Small local theaters sometimes need kid actors—and they may even pay. Plays are hard work but fun—especially at the end when you take your bows in a room full of enthusiastic applause! Visit the theaters in your area to learn how to get involved.

Movies: To learn about auditions in your area, ask the director of your school or community theaters and check your local newspaper for casting calls. Unless you live in a big movie-making area, such as Los Angeles, you're most likely to find work in student or independent films this way. If you're serious about making the break onto the big screen, you should contact some talent agencies to find out how to apply.

TV: Casting calls for TV are advertised much like movies and stage; however, you may also have a shot in ads that businesses in your area will show on local channels. By auditioning for advertisements, you can build your resume for other auditions. Acting in commercials is a great way to make money when first starting in the business. You can find out about auditions for national ads through acting agencies.

Activities That Can Help You Get the Job

Volunteer at local theaters: Even the most successful actors typically begin in companies so small that everyone must do more than one job. Starting your career by painting sets or sewing costumes will provide you with good experience and contacts.

School plays: A school play is one of the best ways to get experience, especially when a lot of high-school plays can be almost professional in quality. Most of the stars you hear about were acting in their school plays, too. It's a terrific way to get involved!

Usher: Work at a local theater as an usher. You can get discounts on tickets or free admission to the plays. What could be better if you love theater?

Theater groups: Is a theater group in your city performing a play? They often need teenagers for unpaid bit parts. Work your way up. Of course, if you happen to live in New York City, you can go out and audition right now!

Movie extras: When a movie is being made in your area, sometimes the production company will put out a call for extras. This usually involves no pay and lots of waiting around. On the plus side, there can be free food, sightings of famous actors, and, of course, the thrill of watching the cameras in action and maybe even catching sight of yourself on the big screen when the movie comes out. (See that red blur? That's me!)

Internships: Intern with a local theater company to help with stage work; believe me, they always need it. You may not get paid—in fact, you probably won't—but you'll meet a lot of people who can help you along the way.

CHAPTER 14

Computers

PROGRAMMING AND DESIGN

You're sitting in front of a computer, playing your favorite video game, and you're getting paid for it! Who'd have thought that you'd be able to yell back to your mom, "Sorry, I can't empty the trash right now; I'm working!" while you tried to reach Level 17?

Life as a Computer Programmer

Want to create games for Nintendo? Jobs with computers can range from creating a Web site for your friend's company to testing the next new video game. With the constant changes in computer technology, there are no age limits for the people involved in this field. From critiquing video games to designing your own, computers offer teens a way to make money simply for having fun.

Cool Jobs in Computing

Webmaster: Web design is one way that teenagers have made a ton of money in the last couple years. Do you understand HTML and Javascript? Even if you don't, you can still create Web sites. Most often businesses pay for this. The biggest market for teen Web masters is small businesses because they're willing to take a chance if you charge less. Once you've built up your credentials by designing Web sites for smaller businesses, larger companies might pay you to do the same. Contacts are everything in this business; the key is getting your first job. Look at listings of small businesses and find out if they have Web sites. If not, create a sample of your work and offer to design their Web site at a reduced price.

Computer retail: What could be better than working around the games you want to create? Get a job in a computer game or electronics store. Imagine the discounts on games! Getting this job is similar to getting other retail jobs: walk in, apply for a job, maybe interview, and, if you're hired, begin to work! You probably have a favorite game store; start by applying there. The fact that you're a regular customer may help you get the job.

Computer customer service: You will need a LOT of patience for this job. Get ready to explain the same thing over and over, teach people how to use their computers correctly, and answer their questions. You can get this job by applying for a job at a computer store. If you have some knowledge of how computers work, tell the manager, and most likely you'll be rerouted to working in customer assistance.

Video game tester: You can also earn money testing new versions of games that big companies are bringing out. You'll need to contact the companies that produce games, like Nintendo, Microsoft, or Sony, to see if they're looking for video game testers.

Game reviewer: This is the perfect job if you are obsessed with gaming. If you love gaming and like to write, think about reviewing video games. You'll get free copies of the games to review, spend some time playing them, write up a review of it, and earn money. You can also save yourself a lot of money by not wasting it on games you end up hating. Contact a gaming magazine and ask them about writing reviews. Send them a sample review of a video game you really like and one of a game you really dislike.

Computer teacher/aid: Computer classes are set up for people who need to learn how to use a computer. You'll teach them how to perform basic tasks like word processing, going on the Internet, and e-mailing. Go to a community center and see if they need someone to teach computer classes. Once you get started, write lesson plans and have a good idea of what you want to cover in each class. If a community center doesn't need you, try contacting a senior center. Right now there are a lot of seniors who want to learn how to use the latest technology.

Activities That Can Help You Get the Job

Take computer classes: Go to a local community college and find out what programming courses they have, then take them! Or start taking some classes in computer repair. Your school may have computer classes or a teacher whom you could assist in the computer lab.

Test games for free: Find a game producer and offer to be a tester—free of charge. Tell them about your invaluable knowledge of gaming and programming, as well as your devotion to their particular games. Once you've done this, you'll have plenty to show a magazine, newspaper, or Web site when you start submitting reviews.

Join or start a gaming club at school: You can get together with other gamers, talk about various games, and, if they have other gaming systems, you can all make deals so that you yourself won't have to pay hundreds of dollars for systems to test games on.

Volunteer to fix old computers: You can gain experience working with computers by fixing or recycling old ones. Many schools and youth organizations sponsor programs that allow students to get hands-on experience in computer repair.

Internships: Any company that deals with computers is a good place for an internship. If you're interested in Web design, you can also contact the web-master of a local business's Web site to see if he needs any help maintaining that Web site.

Apprenticeships: You can also try an apprenticeship with someone who fixes computers. If you can, find an adult computer tech and see if a) she can teach you anything or b) set you up with some companies who could use your help.

CHAPTER 15

Fashion

FROM OLD NAVY TO SAKS FIFTH AVENUE

You live at the mall. You've been known to envy mannequins for getting to spend 24 hours a day in clothing stores. You've been browsing Teen People's *fashion section since you could read. Well, maybe you're not quite that addicted to fashion, but you love it!*

The Life of a Fashion Designer

Guess what! For once, loving clothes could actually earn you money instead of costing money. Have you ever noticed a great shirt or a pair of pants that were insanely expensive and thought, "Hey, I could make that—and I could make it look even better!" You probably could; after all, you know what you like to wear and you know what your friends like. Basically, a fashion designer creates new pieces of clothing or jewelry and then sells them directly to people . . . people like you and your friends!

Teen Jobs for the Fashionably Creative

Retail: Work at your favorite clothing store. What could be more obvious? You get paid (and get a discount!) and the store owners gets an employee who loves their clothes. Everybody wins.

Modeling: Maybe you've dreamed of being a teen model, featured in your favorite magazines, wearing thousand-dollar shirts and two-thousand-dollar pants. Contact local modeling agencies in your area to learn how you can get started.

Fabric store: Learn about the best fabric for your new clothing designs and get great discounts on patterns! You'll get a feel for which fabrics last, which ones fall apart, how to sew the various kinds of cloth . . . everything you need to know about the stuff that makes the clothes.

Start your own clothing company: You and your friends will love showing off all of your latest designs at school. Since they're your own creations, you can be sure no one else will be wearing the same outfit as you. You're also in complete control from the cut of the clothes to the type of cloth. Tell me there hasn't been a time when you've thought, "Hey, those jeans would be perfect if they just . . . " Well, here's your chance to make it so that your jeans are perfect!

Activities That Can Help You Get the Job

Costume director: Want to try that crazy new fabric you saw, but you're too shy to wear it yourself? Put it in a costume! Plays are a great creative outlet for the sewing savvy. You get to design and create your own visions, and of course, the play provides instant publicity for your outfits. Designing costumes for the school play may not seem glamorous, but it's a start.

Sewing club: If you really like sewing, start a sewing club or enter a sewing contest. It's a useful skill for everything from repairing your favorite pair of jeans to learning how to make your own clothes.

Volunteer at Goodwill: Before you get too far into daydreaming about your fashion design career, imagine what it would be like to not be able to afford the clothes you want to wear. Volunteer with a program that collects used clothing, like Goodwill. You'll get to be around clothes, plus you'll be helping out the community. That funky '70s shirt in "the bins" could inspire some fashion creativity.

Internships: A fashion internship might not seem like it has much to do with designing clothes, but it's the best way to get contacts and ideas for your new clothing line. For example, intern with the fashion department of a teen magazine or clothing store. You'll get to be around some great clothes (without paying a cent) and benefit from the vast knowledge of the fashion savvy. Or intern with a fashion designer. Many start-up designers could use the extra help.

Educate yourself: At school, the best class you can take to get yourself fashion ready would be a home economics class that offers sewing or an art class. Art classes can offer great opportunities to test your creative ideas and fashion designs. For modeling, try theater classes (so you'll be able to relax with everyone staring at you).

CHAPTER 16

Working with Animals

PUPPIES, KITTENS, AND TAME IGUANAS

Ah, another day at work. You pull on some gloves, open the cage, and pull out . . . an iguana?! Yup, not all animals are cute and fuzzy, but you love them all anyway. Today you're volunteering at the local zoo, and then you're off to the stables to train your favorite horse. Well, life is certainly never boring!

The Life of a Veterinarian

There are lots of jobs for people who love all types of animals. Not all veterinarians take care of pets, and not all veterinarians work at clinics. Think driving around in a pickup or a van with all your medical equipment and treating horses, cows, sheep, goats, chickens, geese, llamas . . .

Animal-Related Jobs

Veterinary assistant: Working for a veterinarian, you might end up working as a receptionist, cleaning up after animals, or helping to feed and walk sick animals. But hey, it's still experience. (Just a note—many veterinary clinics have a minimum age requirement. A lot of the time you'll need to be sixteen or over.)

Pet store: Get a job at a pet store, bring a clothespin for your nose, and try not to fall in love with every animal you see. Working at a pet store is a great way to be around animals and share your interest in them with other people. You also might get to clean up after a lot of animals. Apply for this job just like you would for any other retail job—resume/application, interview, and so on.

Zoo worker: Lions, tigers, and bears, oh my! You might get to feed the animals, work in the gift shop, clean up their "habitats," or lead tours. Lots of zoos have camps; you could also be a zoo camp counselor. Head to the zoo and ask at the entrance where you can find information about working there.

Stable hand/riding teacher: This is definitely a job for people who love horses. You get paid and you're always around horses. You could work at a stable, caring for the horses or assisting with riding lessons. To actually assist with riding lessons, you'll need to be able to prove that you've got lots of experience handling horses (it helps if you own one, but it's not a requirement). You can contact boarding stables and horseback riding teachers/ clinics in the phone book and ask if they need an assistant or stable hand.

Activities That Can Help You Get the Job

Animal shelter: If you can bear to do it, your local humane society or animal shelter always needs volunteers. Just try not to get too attached to the animals—you can't take every pet home with you.

Train seeing-eye dogs: Do you want to help people and interact with animals at the same time? Many blind or vision-impaired people rely on seeing-eye dogs to help them with their day-to-day lives. Each dog must first complete a training program run by volunteers. Just be sure your parents can handle you bringing home a dog for a few weeks.

4-H and FFA: Both programs are active in raising farm animals and showing those animals at fairs and national competitions. Getting involved allows teens to build skills as leaders while working with animals.

Internships: If you can't work for a veterinarian, you can certainly intern with him or her. And if you can't intern, you can always job shadow for the day.

CHAPTER 17

The Arts

VAN GOGH WITH BOTH EARS

Your bedroom's painted with murals, but you can't see them because every inch of your wall is covered with your work. The sculpture you just couldn't bear to get rid of has been collecting dust in a corner of your room, but you don't really notice because your next sculpture-in-progress is sitting right in front of it and your chisels are all over the floor. Art is your life.

Life as an Artist

Do you drool over Leonardo (da Vinci, that is), daydream about Michelangelo, and wish you lived in the Louvre? Well, you've chosen the right thing to love, because there are tons of jobs that involve art! As an artist, you can work in painting, drawing, photography, or sculpture. Then you just have to try to figure out ways to sell your work.

Jobs for Your Artistic Side

Graphic designer: A graphic designer creates flyers, logos, and ads. You might work for a toy company, designing the packaging you think will attract kids to the toys. Or you might work for a book publisher, designing book covers and publicity campaigns. You'll need to know how to use the more common graphic design programs, like Quark Xpress, Adobe Photoshop, and Illustrator.

Art supply store: "Can I help you find something? No, I'm sorry, we're out of easels. May I direct you to our fine selection of paints?" Get a job at a place that sells art stuff and you may even get an employee discount on art supplies.

Outdoor artist: Ever watch those people who do paintings in the park or at art fairs? You may not make much money, but you'll gain exposure doing what you love. You need to be good at hawking your work. ("Wouldn't you love to have your portrait painted today? It'll only take ten minutes of your time, but you'll have the painting to keep forever.")

Art teacher: Do you know some special art technique, like calligraphy or clay modeling? Or do you have a great all-around knowledge of art? Teach art classes at a community center to younger kids. You may start out volunteering, but if you stay long enough and everyone loves your classes, you might even get paid.

Activities That Can Help You Get the Job

Art club: Welcome to the Finger-Painting Club! Oh, I'm sorry, brushes won't be allowed, only fingers . . . just kidding. Join an art club at your school or start one. This can be a great opportunity to experiment with other mediums.

Museum volunteer: Get ready to memorize the location of every Van Gogh, Picasso, and Monet, plus where to find the bathrooms and the gift shop. Be a guide at an art museum. Try to pick a place that you already love so your passion will really come through.

Internships: You can intern at an art gallery. A small one is best. Then when you're trying to have your first show, that gallery where you interned is your best chance and you'll have the know-how to do it. Or intern with a PR firm in the graphic design division or at a local art gallery. When you are looking for your first job as a college graduate or for a venue for your first solo art show, the firm will remember you, and your time with them will generate important contacts in the field at large.

School newspaper or art magazine: Join your school newspaper, yearbook, or literary magazine and start working with layout and design. That's the best way to get experience in graphic design. You can also submit your illustrations for publication.

Art classes: Take classes on using various design programs. Experience and knowledge of the programs are a requirement for almost all the graphic design jobs that you can hope to get. Of course, art classes are also great for an introduction to different techniques: sculpture, painting, drawing, and etching, or you can take advanced classes to hone your skills.

Send out your work: It's never too early to begin selling your work. Send sample copies of your artwork to publishers, newspapers, and magazines. If the editors like your work they'll keep it on file and see if something comes up that would work well with your style.

Start your own comic book: Do you have an amazing idea for a superhero? Make up a series and share it with your friends. Cartoonists spend years developing their characters, so the sooner you start the better. (Read the book *So, You Wanna Be A Comic Book Artist?* for more information!)

School newspaper cartoonist: Start drawing cartoons for your school newspaper. You won't get paid, but you'll get exposure, and soon the entire class, if not the entire school, will know you as "the kid who draws cartoons for the newspaper."

CHAPTER 18

Sports

GOALS, TOUCHDOWNS, AND THE 4-MINUTE MILE

So you love sports. You're the goalie for the soccer team, quarterback for the football team, All-State tennis champion, and now you'd like to get paid for it. Don't worry, there are plenty of sports jobs for you to choose from! Now picture this: waking up to a two-hour warm-up and soccer practice, knowing that tomorrow you'll be playing in the Olympics! Sound fun?

Life in Professional Sports

Do you love catcher's mitts, new soccer balls, fencing foils, and volleyball nets? Feel like spending your summer (or fall or winter or spring) around that $400 snowboard? You play sports, work with sports, live sports, breathe sports, eat sports (well, maybe not). There are lots of sports jobs to consider. Baseball, football, soccer, fencing, volleyball, snowboarding, skiing, bicycling . . . almost anything that involves a verb, you can call it a sport, and you can make it your job.

Jobs for the Teen Athlete in You

Referee: Referees are sometimes not the most-loved person on the field, but they have a really important job. As a teen, you can referee kids' games. You will want to stick to a sport that you're particularly knowledgeable about. Go to the league organizers and ask how to apply for a job as a referee.

Coach: You're always playing sports, but for once you have a little bit of control over what happens. Coaching a kids' team gives you great experience, and you'll get to teach kids how to love sports. You'll run through the exercises you know by heart and give the kids the benefit of your expertise.

Sports store: Working at a sporting-goods store, you'll gain knowledge from expert employees and customers on all kinds of equipment. You'll also have the first look at the latest gear for whatever sports interest you. Best of all, there's usually a discount.

Golf caddy: "Caddy, bring me my three-wood!" Eager to hear those words often? Get a job as a caddy at a golf club. It's great for your arm strength, and you'll learn more about how to improve your golf swing so that you can become the next Tiger Woods.

Sports camp: Feel like an intense two or three weeks of sports? Be a counselor at a summer sports camp. It's like coaching a team multiplied by 35 and crammed into two weeks.

Sports endorsements: Are you an awesome snowboarder or water-skier who competes regularly? See if you can get an endorsement from a local sporting-goods company.

Activities That Can Help You Get the Job

Volunteer: Any big sports events coming to your city? Lucky you. Contact the organizers to find out if they need volunteers.

Special Olympics volunteer: Contact the Special Olympics for information on volunteering. It's not a paying job, but you get to help kids and get a huge boost on both your resume and your college applications.

School sports: Go, team, go! Get used to hearing it or saying it. Join a school sports team or cheerleading squad and gain more knowledge about the games you love.

Ball boy (or girl): Want a taste of fame and fortune without working for it too much? Get a job as a ball boy or bat boy for your city's professional sports team. Contact your city's team and ask if they need help.

School sports announcer: See if you can volunteer to be a sports announcer for high school or middle school games. The school may or may not pay you, but it's a good way to get sports-related job experience.

CHAPTER 19

Food

PIZZA TO PETIT FOURS

You work in a four-star restaurant that people come from around the world to eat at. Your pasta dishes are legend, and your desserts have been known to make people faint with happiness. You love food!

Life in the Food Industry

Do you love food, eating it, making it, sharing its delicious wonders with other people? Working in the restaurant industry, you might take orders, bus tables, prep food for cooking, and take money (including, hopefully, large tips).

Fun Food Jobs

Waiter: Look around your favorite restaurants and see how old the waiters are. Teenagers? People in their mid-twenties? Adults? When you're looking for your first job as a waiter, go for a restaurant where the other waiters are about your age. Interested in tips and actual meals? Get a job at a real restaurant, and remember: the more the food costs, the higher the tips are.

Restaurant host/hostess: "How many in your party tonight?" Hosting is a great way to break into the restaurant business. You don't need all the experience waiters do—just great social skills. Taking reservations and showing people to their tables doesn't earn the big tips, but it's a way to get your name in with the manager.

Coffee shop or deli: This includes working at Starbucks, working at a bagel place, or working in an actual deli. You stand at the counter, take orders, make the food, give the order to one of your coworkers, and give the food/drink to the customer. While you're working you'll learn all about great, delicious specialty foods and how to make them.

Activities That Can Help You Get the Job

Cooking classes: Check your local newspaper for listings of cooking classes. They range from basic, this-is-how-you-turn-on-the-oven classes to cake-decorating and mousse-making classes. Mmmmm . . . just imagine tasting all that great food!

Making family meals: Volunteer to cook dinner once in a while! You can't exactly put it on your resume, but it'll give you a feel for how long it takes to cook certain dishes and exactly how forgiving various kinds of fruit are. Plus, your family will be a lot more likely to appreciate all the effort that you put into dinner.

Soup kitchens: This is a terrific way to get experience around food and help the community at the same time. It gives you that nice, warm, fuzzy feeling (like eating a bowl of chicken soup, incidentally), and it's great on your resume and college apps.

CHAPTER 20

Film

SMILE, YOU'RE ON CAMERA!

And the Oscar goes to . . . you! All your hard work has finally paid off! You slaved for months over the screenplay, the production, the funding, the casting, the shooting, the music, the editing, etc., and now you're reaping the rewards. Just think, it all started with your love of film.

The Life of a Filmmaker

Do you daydream about being the next Steven Spielberg? Peter Jackson? George Lucas? Maybe you don't like the movies that people make right now, and you'd like to make your own. That's what a filmmaker does. You choose the actors and actresses, figure out how you want the film to be shot, and do publicity for your movie.

Film-Related Jobs

Movie theater: Sell tickets, take tickets, sell popcorn, sweep up popcorn, mop the bathrooms, clean the theaters between each showing . . . and get discounts on tickets! Plus, if you work at a small, artsy movie theater, you can use your connections there later on to get your movie shown!

Video rental store: This is a great job if you've seen lots of movies, because people will ask your opinion on different movies that they want to rent, and you might get discounts on all the new movies coming in.

Photo lab or studio: You know how one of the best parts of a trip is getting back all the photos you took? Add to that joy by being the one developing those photos. You can also learn more about developing film.

Activities That Can Help You Get the Job

Enter your movie into a film festival: Start making movies and entering them into film festivals. It's the best way to get your name out there and have people start noticing you as an aspiring director/producer. There are film festivals all over; some of them even take submissions from those under 18. There is usually an entry fee, and sometimes your film has to be nominated for the festival, rather than you just entering it. But film festivals are where a lot of directors get their start.

Film classes: Take film classes. Many art centers and community colleges have them. These classes can show you how to make better movies and how the film industry works.

Intern at a film studio: Try to get an internship with a film studio; it can be anywhere from a small commercial studio to something like Miramax, Universal Studios, or Disney. You'll make connections so that when you finish your first movie, you'll know some people who can help you.

Screenwriting: You'll need two things: creativity and the dedication to re-write draft after draft. After pitching your idea to studio head, you'll retain a lot of creative license in moving the story the way you want, but remember, the directors, producers, and even the cast will all want to have their say.

TV at school: Dream of starring in your own soap opera? Start at school. Many schools or community centers have media equipment and classes to help you learn how to operate cameras, sound equipment, and everything in the editing room. Some places even have their own local access channels where you can air your creations.

Find a mentor: Is there a local photographer or filmmaker whose work you really admire? Arrange a mentorship with them. Benefit from their knowledge on everything from cameras to zoom shots.

CHAPTER 21

Job Resources

GREAT JOB-SEARCHING INFO

By now you should have an idea of how to read the classifieds, write a resume, have a great interview, and find a job that you really feel passionate about, whether it's in film or writing or sports or performing. Just in case you didn't find what your looking for in this book, here are a few resources to give you the best shot possible at getting your dream job. Good luck and happy job hunting!

Job-Searching Resources

www.youthgig.com
This Web site lists various part-time jobs available for teenagers. Employers can post job openings online, and teenagers can post want ads on the site for employers to search. Every day the site showcases a "featured employer" for teens, such as IHOP.

www.juniorjobs.com
Junior Jobs features a job listing site for the DC area but also provides job tips and information on grants for young entrepreneurs.

www.studentjobs.gov
Student Jobs is a job/internship connection site for teens and the Federal

Government. Teens can create a profile/resume, search for government jobs, and learn more about working in the government.

www.jobsearch.about.com/cs/justforstudents/
This Web site includes tips for finding a job, such as how to write a resume and cover letter. Also provides links to other teen job sites. Outlines the labor laws as well.

www.youthrules.dol.gov/jobs.htm
Youth Rules focuses on U.S. Department of Labor child labor laws and breaks down the jobs available for kids according to age group. The Web site also provides links for the rules for specialized jobs, such as working on a farm, and lists jobs that are prohibited for certain ages.

www.jobprofiles.org
This site features profiles of experienced workers who share information about their jobs, including the rewards, the stressful parts, the basic skills needed, the future challenges they face, and their advice on entering that particular career.

www.jobdoggy.com
Job Doggy offers tips about summer jobs for teens, as well as a guide that will help them write a resume.

www.teens4hire.com
If you are 14 years old and up, you can use this site to create a profile, search jobs, and apply for work online.

www.snagajob.com
Snagajob provides a search engine so that teens can search for part-time and hourly jobs. The site also allows teens to search by job category, zip code, city, and state.

www.campjobs.com

This site helps teens to find jobs at a summer camps. It allows teens the ability to learn more about different camps, post their resume, and ask questions about camp positions.

www.jobgusher.com

JobGusher.com allows teens to search for a job by typing in their job skills, a job type, or a company they would like to work for. Resumes can be posted, and jobs listings can be viewed as well.

www.groovejob.com

This site focuses on jobs for students. Thousands of jobs for high school and college students can be searched here. There is also a resume builder and interview tips.

www.dollardiva.com

A Web site for women and girl entrepreneurs that features tips on building a business. The company also sponsors a newsletter and nationwide programs.

www.fabjob.com

Fab Job has information on many "fab" careers and features corresponding books (available for purchase) that offer more tips for landing the job.

www.teachingkidsbusiness.com/kidse-marketplace.htm

This site has good information on jobs for kids and teens under 18 years old, and encourages young people to start up their own businesses.

www.osha.gov/SLTC/teenworkers/employers.html

A government site that provides info on workplace laws and standards at the Federal and State level. OSHA also has great ideas to help you stay safe while on the job.

Bibliography

Adams, Bob. *The Everything Job Interview Book*. Avon, MA: Adams Media Corporation, 2001.

Allen, Jeffrey G. *The Complete Q&A Job Interview Book*. New York: John Wiley & Sons, 2000.

Asher, Donald. *Overnight Job Change Strategy*. Berkeley, CA: Ten Speed Press, 1993.

Barkley, Nella. *How to Help Your Child Land the Right Job (without Being a Pain in the Neck)*. New York: Workman Publishing, 1993.

Bloch, Deborah. *How to Have a Winning Job Interview*. Chicago: NTC/Contemporary Publishing Group, 1998.

"Cover Letters and Other Business Correspondence." www.upenn.edu/careerservices/wharton/coverlet_wharton.htm. (11 September 2002).

"Discover the Work You Were Born to Do." Editorial.careers.msn.com/articles/born (9 September 2002).

Eyler, David R. *The Ultimate Job Book*. Revised and Updated Edition. New York: Random House Trade Paperbacks, 2002.

Fry, Ron. *Your First Interview*. 4th ed. Franklin Lakes, NJ: Career Press, 1995.

Fry, Ron. *Your First Resume*. 5th ed. Franklin Lakes, NJ: Career Press; 2001.

"The Five Worst Jobs for Teens," www.familyeducation.com (6 September 2002).

Gottesman, Deb. *The Interview Rehearsal Book: 7 Steps to Job Winning Interviews Using Acting Skills You Never Knew You Had.* Berkeley: Berkeley Publishing Group, 1999.

Graber, Steven. *The Everything Cover Letter Book.* New York: Adams Business Media, 2000.

Graber, Steven. *The Everything Resume Book.* Avon, MA: Adams Media Corporation, 2000.

"Internships. How to Find an Internship." www.jobsearch.about.com/library/weekly/aa081802a.htm (11 September 2002)

Ireland, Susan. *Complete Idiot's Guide to the Perfect Resume.* Indianapolis: Alpha Books, 2003.

Kennedy, Joyce Lain. *Resumes for Dummies.* 4th ed. New York: John Wiley & Sons, 2002.

Krannich, Caryl and Ron Krannich. *Savvy Interviewing: The Nonverbal Advantage.* Manassas Park, VA: Impact Publications, 2000.

Krannich, Caryl and Ron Krannich. *Dynamite Cover Letters.* Manassas Park, VA: Impact Publications, 1999.

Orsborn, Carol. *How Would Confucius Ask for a Raise?* New York: William Morrow and Company, 1994.

Pervola, Cindy. *How to Get a Job If You're a Teenager.* 2nd ed. Highsmith Press, 2000.

Rosenburg, Arthur D. *The Resume Handbook.* Avon, Mass.: Adams Media Corporation, 1996.

"So. . . You Want to be a Star? Arts and Entertainment Jobs." www.jobsearch.about.com/library/weekly/aa071401a.htm (11 September 2002).

"State Labor Law Summaries," www.snagajob.com/labor_laws.asp (11 September 2002).

Troutman, Kathryn K. *Creating Your High School Resume.* Indianapolis: Jist Works, 1998.

"Youth Rules." www.youthrules.dol.gov (12 May 2003).

Vernon, Naomi. *A Teen's Guide to Finding a Job.* New York: 1st Books Library, 2003.

Veruki, Peter. *The 250 Job Interview Questions You'll Most Likely Be Asked.* Avon, MA: Adams Media Corporation, 1999.

Wendleton, Kate. *Building a Great Resume.* 2nd ed. Franklin Lakes, NJ: Career Press, 1999.

Acknowledgements

Thanks to my wonderful editor Barbara, for hours of work, and to everyone else at Beyond Words. Thanks to my parents for their continued support of me and my writing, from chauffeuring me around to letting me skip chores "just this once." And finally, thanks to Michelle Roehm McCann, for taking a chance on a twelve-year-old.